authentic influence

leading without titles

Tim Elmore

foreword by John Maxwell

LifeWay Press
Nashville, Tennessee

Published by:

National Collegiate Ministry

LifeWay Christian Resources

127 Ninth Avenue North

Nashville, TN 37234

Customer Service: (800) 458-2772

Order additional copies of this book by writing to Customer Service Center, MSN 113;

127 Ninth Avenue, North; Nashville, TN 37234-0113; by calling toll free (800) 458-2772;

by faxing (615) 251-5933; by ordering online at www.lifeway.com;

by emailing customerservice@lifeway.com; or by visiting a LifeWay Christian Store.

Printed in The United States of America

ISBN 0-6330-1902-X

EQUIP   LifeWay Christian Resources

PO Box 7700   127 Ninth Avenue, North

Atlanta, GA 30338   Nashville, TN 37234-0151

As God works through us, we will help people and churches know Jesus Christ and seek His kingdom

by providing biblical solutions that spiritually transform individuals and cultures.

Contents

Acknowledgments

I have to thank the team of leaders that National Collegiate Ministry assembled under Bill Henry for their invaluable input in the creation of this resource. These men and women from all over the country shared their wisdom and experience in an effort to produce the best tool possible for developing emerging leaders.

I also wish to thank Tracey Fries, my executive assistant, who helped me reach goals I could not have reached without help. She protects me and provides for me so that I can focus on creating resources.

Finally, I wish to thank my friend and comrade Janise Matyas Smith, who labored with me to create this guide. She worked with diligence and detail until it was finished. Thanks Janise for modeling the skills we try to communicate in this resource.

Foreword

I have seen the need for leadership development since I was a college student in the 1960s. I only wish someone had handed me a guide book like this one to help me interpret situations, relate to people and achieve goals. To be honest, I never received any leadership training in a college classroom. I recognized my need to become a leader once I launched my career and had no tools to help me do it.

This is why EQUIP and National Collegiate Ministry are partnering together. We are committed to walk alongside Christian universities and college ministries to give you the tools now. We want to add value to your life and ministry. We know many ministries are committed to teaching leadership, and we simply want to be part of the process. I founded EQUIP in 1996 because I saw some strategic arenas in need of practical tools in this subject area. College students were one of my driving motivations to build a team and create new resources. I want to help your generation lead effectively without having to make all the mistakes my generation made.

There are six conclusions we have drawn as we have ministered to collegians:
1. Leaders are made, not born.
2. Every collegian has leadership potential.
3. Collegians learn leadership best in communities.
4. Leadership development is a process, not an event.
5. In today's world, every collegian will need to learn leadership.
6. College students need a coach to help them grow into effective leaders.

I am excited about this partnership. The guidebook will be part of the coaching process. I trust you will become a student of leadership for life. Leadership development is a marathon, not a sprint. Get involved in a mentoring/covenant group. Reflect on the questions and discuss what you are learning.

I think you will enjoy this resource. Tim Elmore has served on my staff since 1983. He has worked with college students even longer and is able to help you wrap your arms around the subject of leadership. I have had the privilege of mentoring him, and commend him as a mentor to you. I hope you enjoy the leadership journey. I pray you grow into a person of authentic influence.

Blessings on you as you develop as a leader,

Dr. John C. Maxwell
Founder, Injoy/EQUIP

God Never Calls a Wrong Number

HOW GOD CALLS A LEADER

"Then I heard the voice of the Lord saying, 'Whom shall I send? And who will go for us?' And I said, 'Here I am. Send me!'" Isaiah 6:8.

"The word of the Lord came to me, saying, 'Before I formed you in the womb I knew you, before you were born I set you apart; I appointed you as a prophet to the nations'" Jeremiah 1:4–5.

Are You Listening?

In the late 1800s, a group of young job seekers congregated in the waiting room of a telegraph hiring agency. Each job prospect who was waiting for an interview was engulfed in reading, chatting and munching . . . except one young man. Through all the commotion he heard a message tapped out in code, "If you hear this message, come through the office door." With ears perked up, the man understood the invitation being offered. So the young man walked through the office door. A few minutes later he returned to the waiting room, grinned and told the other job seekers, "You can all go home, I just got the job."

Like the prophet Isaiah (Is. 6:1–8), this young man heard the general call that went out to everyone in the waiting room, and responded to it, making it his call. He listened. He understood. He acted. He got results.

Wrong Number?

Wrong numbers are dialed millions of times each day across the United States. But how do you know it's a wrong number? What's your first clue? Have you ever thought about how you draw the conclusion that they have the wrong number?
1. First, you don't recognize the other person's voice.
2. Second, they ask for someone you don't recognize.
3. Third, the subject they bring up doesn't make sense or seem relevant to you.

Often when God calls us, we are tempted to treat it like a wrong number for the same reasons. His call seems strange. It feels like it is for someone else. But it is not! As a result of this lesson, many of us will realize that God has placed a call on our lives that we must respond to, now. A call to serve is a call to prepare.

The Fact of the Matter

You can lead now! God often calls us as young people to serve, and we don't have to wait to make a major impact on our world. Remember 1 Timothy 4:12, "Don't let anyone think less of you because you are young, but be an example . . . " (NLT).

Basic Truth
You will become what you are becoming right now.

Guided Prayer
Dear God,
it is my desire to know Your will and the call You have placed upon my life.

Open my heart to receive Your truth.

Open my ears to hear Your voice.

Open my eyes to see Your face.

May I respond in obedience and surrender.

May I be an instrument of Your grace and love.

Amen.

Born to Lead

Consider this. The first description of mankind we find in the Bible has to do with leadership. God designed us to lead, have authority and take dominion. According to Genesis 1:26-31, you and I were born to lead! Take a look at five observations based on this text that give us a glimpse of our God-given leadership potential.

⚙ **Being made in God's image means we were created to lead and rule. v. 26**
God said, "Let us make man in our image…" What does this mean? The next phrase gives us a clue: "…and let him rule." Part of what it means to be like God is that we were given the potential to lead the earth. If it is His intention for us to do this, He must have also given us the capacity to do it. God equips those whom He calls.

⚙ **God commanded both males and females to have dominion. v. 27**
This verse reminds us that both males and females were made in His image. Leadership gifts, roles and calling are not gender exclusive. Both men and women have the potential to lead and influence others. The two genders may approach leadership differently, but this means we can learn something about God's leadership from each one.

⚙ **We are to rule over the earth, but not over each other. v. 28**
Humans were not given authority to rule over each other. History is the story of how we have perverted this call to rule and take dominion. People have attempted to dominate each other instead of finding out what God means by leading and ruling. We were told to take dominion over the earth and its creatures, not over other humans.

⚙ **All of creation is to serve each other in the area of their gift and purpose. vv. 29-30**
Everything was created for a purpose, from the grass to the cattle. If God's purpose is for humans to lead the rest of creation, then He must have given us the tools to do so. Our purpose then should be to ask: Lord, what is my specific purpose? Where is my area of dominion in which I can serve?

⚙ **Our leadership is best exercised in the area of our giftedness. v.31**
God said that His creation was good. When people discover their gifts and function in them, they will naturally lead in those areas. When we find our purpose and our gift, we naturally influence. It is then that we are most productive, most intuitive, most comfortable and most satisfied. So, our goal is not to dominate, but to find our purpose and serve!

Reflect and Respond...

We are often intimidated by the idea of leadership. Can you see that God's perspective is quite different than the world's perspective? How do these scriptural observations liberate you to pursue leadership?

Reflect

and

Respond

WAYS THAT GOD CALLS A LEADER

Now that we've seen God's general call on all of our lives, let's examine God's specific calling. In the Bible, we see at least four different ways that God "called" people into their life-purpose. His calling unfolded just as it does for you as a college student today.

Thunderbolt

Example: Apostle Paul
This is the call that we all pray for – it's unmistakable. It's a thunderbolt. Paul experienced this call as he was on the road to Damascus. God spoke, the bright light shone, and Paul's life was changed forever. These calls often occur as a "crisis event" in a moment or a season of our lives when we suddenly know what to do. It might happen in a worship service or one night when we're praying, and our lives are changed forever. However it occurs, the call comes clearly.

Walking Through Open Doors

Example: Queen Esther
This call comes over time. It is a progressive revelation, one step at a time. Esther, the queen of Persia in the Old Testament, simply made wise, God-honoring decisions that eventually saved her fellow Jews from annihilation. She was a beautiful Jewish girl that was picked as queen in a foreign land. She earned influence with the king and built relationships with those around her. While she was queen, Mordecai, her mentor, discovered a conspiracy against her people. Esther responded by simply obeying God and taking the steps of opportunity along the way. Her steps didn't seem big at the time and her call didn't make sense until it all came together in the end.

Call From Birth

Example: Jeremiah
Those whom God has called from birth have known their calling ever since they can remember. (They might not have responded to the call, but they know that they've been called). When Jeremiah was only a young man, God called and informed him that he was going to tear down nations and setup other nations. Jeremiah told God that he was too young for the work. Yet God reassured Jeremiah of His intentions: "Before you were born I set you apart and appointed you as my spokesman to the world" (Jer. 1:5, NLT).

Growing Awareness

Example: Joseph
This kind of call comes early, but only in a very general way. Those who have a growing awareness of their calling begin to understand that something is happening and start sifting through it early on in life. Even though they know "something is there," they don't fully comprehend what God has for them until they mature. Unlike "walking through open doors," when his call came, Joseph understood the "big picture" up front, as a teenager. What he didn't understand were the details. He realized them along the way. Joseph began his life with a leadership dream (the early sense of a call), then he was sold into slavery and thrown into prison. All of this led up to his being put second in command of Egypt. As you read about Joseph's life in Genesis, you realize that he had a growing awareness that God was fulfilling the dream as he matured, filling in the details along the way.

Have you ever experienced God's call on your life? If you don't believe that you have, you will learn more about what this means in this session. If you have experienced such a calling, describe the experience below. What evidence have you seen to reinforce the call? Can you identify with any of the four ways God called people in Scripture? Respond with your experience if you can in the space allotted.

Reflect and Respond

Group Up

Share your experience of God's call on your life.

Explain to the group what process God went through to reveal His calling to you.

DAVID'S CALL

King David, a man after God's own heart, was called to lead an entire nation while he was still in his teens. Although he was the least likely of his family to be crowned as king, God chose to call him anyway. And David led God's people to unprecedented spiritual and military prosperity.

Read 1 Samuel 16:1, 6-13. In this passage, we get to look in on David's call from God and his anointing by the prophet Samuel. There are three important truths we learn from David's call. These truths can also impact us.

1. God chose David to be a leader even when others put "lids" on him.

Neither Jesse, David's family, Saul, or Goliath believed in David's leadership.

- **His dad didn't even ask him to come in from the field to be considered.**
  The first time it happened, David's father put a lid on David.

  "So he asked Jesse, 'Are these all the sons you have?' 'There is still the youngest,' Jesse answered, 'but he is tending the sheep'" (1 Sam. 16:11).

  Even Jesse, David's own father, was saying, "You're too young. You're just a shepherd. You just don't seem tough enough. Surely you won't be the next king of Israel."

- **His brothers rebuked him when he visited them on the battlefield.**
  Eliab, David's brother, was the second person to put a lid on him.

  "When Eliab, David's oldest brother, heard him speaking with the men, he burned with anger at him and asked, 'Why have you come down here? And with whom did you leave those few sheep in the desert? I know how conceited you are and how wicked your heart is; you came down only to watch the battle'" (1 Sam. 17:28).

  Eliab was telling David, "You can't help us. You're too young and irresponsible for us. We're too busy for you."

- **King Saul didn't believe in him and thought he could only succeed with the king's armor.**
  David's family members were not the only ones who did not believe in him. Saul, the king of Israel also didn't believe that he could succeed on his own.

  "Saul replied, 'You are not able to out out against this Philistine and fight him; you are only a boy, and he has been a fighting man from his youth.' Then Saul dressed David in his own tunic . He put a coat of armor on him and a bronze helmet on his head" (1 Sam. 17:33,38).

  Saul was basically saying to him, "You're too young. Goliath is experienced. If you do go, do it my way in my armor. It's your only hope of survival."

- **Goliath thought David was a joke and never took him seriously.**
  Not only did David's friends put a lid on his ability, so did his enemies.

  "Meanwhile, the Philistine, with his shield bearer in front of him, kept coming closer to David. He looked David over and saw that he was only a boy., ruddy and handsome, and he despised him. He said to David, 'Am I a dog, that you come at me with sticks?' And the Philistine cursed David by his gods. 'Come here,' he said, 'and I'll give our flesh to the birds of the air and the beasts of the field'" (1 Sam. 17:41-44).

  Goliath mocked David by saying he looked young, fair, and "soft." He taunted him and then cussed him out!

Reflect and Respond...

Have others ever told you that you couldn't do something even though you believed that you could? Have you been denied an opportunity because others didn't believe that you could handle it? Have others not taken you seriously despite the fact that you believed God had called you to do something? Describe how lids have been placed on you.

Reflect

and

Respond

Group Up

As a group, explore how David responded to the lids placed on him.

Refer to 1 Samuel 16-17 to get a more detailed picture of his response.

2. God looked at David's heart and knew his faith and passion were genuine.

Even though others put "lids" on him, God chose David to be a leader. Unlike humans who look for skill, talent, brains, or strength, God looked at David's heart and saw that his faith and passion were genuine. This is what God looks for in a leader.

- **David's faith was in God, not in his own abilities.**
  David had seen God's faithfulness demonstrated in previous times of his life, so he had faith that God would continue to be faithful.

  "The Lord who delivered me from the paw of the lion and the paw of the bear will deliver me from the hand of this Philistine" (1 Sam. 17:37, NIV).

Group Up

Discuss as a group ways that you can cultivate a heart like David.

How can you be a person after God's own heart?

- **David's passion was for God's Kingdom, not his own.**
David didn't desire to take the challenge of fighting the Philistine to prove his abilities or to prove to Israel that he was a leader. Instead, he realized that Goliath was defying God and someone needed to do something about it.

"David said to the Philistine, 'You come against me with sword and spear and javelin, but I come against you in the name of the Lord Almighty, the God of the armies of Israel, whom you have defied'" (1 Sam. 17:45).

- **David's vision was to make God known to the world.**
When David saw Goliath, he didn't just see the challenge; he saw how God could gain glory by the situation.

"This day the Lord will hand you over to me...and the whole world will know that there is a God in Israel" (1 Sam. 17:46).

- **David's heart was like God's heart.**
Early in his life, David cultivated intimacy with God. When he was only a youth, God purposely chose him as king because of his godly heart.

"The Lord has sought out a man after His own heart and appointed him leader of His people" (1 Sam. 13:14).

Reflect and Respond...

If God were to search your inmost being - your deepest thoughts, motivations, and desires - would He describe you as a person after His own heart? Write what characteristics you think would make you this kind of person.

3. God called David as a teen for the same reasons he calls us today.

David was 15 when he was anointed King of Israel. He must have felt inadequate. Most of us at 15 years old are only concerned about fitting in and not embarrassing ourselves. Many of us have wondered at some point: "Why would God call me to be a leader? What do I have to offer? I'm no Billy Graham. I still feel like a kid who's trying to figure out who God is and where my life should go. I have more questions than answers."

This is exactly why God wants to use us. We can be molded. We are dependent upon Him. We know we can't do it by ourselves. We don't have the money, brains, network, power or confidence to try it on our own.

David's early call in life is not an exception to the way that God works. David was only one of many young leaders God called early in life. God called some of the great leaders in the Bible, as well as many of the greatest leaders throughout history, at an early age.

- **Jeremiah**

Jeremiah was God's spokesman to Judah. For 40 years he boldly and courageously proclaimed God's message to God's people. But he was called and he began his public ministry at a young age.

"The Lord gave me a message. He said, 'I knew you before I formed you in your mother's womb. Before you were born I set you apart and appointed you as my spokesman to the world.'"

"'O Sovereign Lord,' I said, 'I can't speak for you! I'm too young!' 'Don't say that,' the Lord replied, 'for you must go wherever I send you and say whatever I tell you. And don't be afraid of the people, for I will be with you and take care of you. I, the Lord, have spoken'" (Jer. 1:4-8, NLT).

- **Samuel**

Samuel was called while he was still a boy serving in the temple.

After Hannah gave her son to the Lord, Samuel grew up in the temple. Eli taught him, as a young child, everything he should know about serving the Lord (1 Sam. 3:10).

- **Josiah**

Josiah became king when he was only eight years old! And he is remembered for obeying God completely in his leadership. He was used by God to purge Israel of idolatry when he was only 20 years old!

"Josiah was eight years old when he became king, and he reigned in Jerusalem for thirty-one years...He did what was pleasing in the Lord's sight and followed the example of his ancestor David. He did not turn aside from doing what was right" (2 Kings 22:1-2, NLT).

- **Timothy**

Timothy was one of Paul's closest companions. He was called to be a church leader while he was still young.

"Don't let anyone think less of you because you are young. Be an example to all believers in what you teach, in the way you live, in your love, your faith and your purity" (1 Tim. 4:12, NLT).

- **Jesus' Disciples**

God called James and John at an early age to follow him. These two disciples, along with Simon Peter, made up Jesus' inner circle of friends.

"A little farther up the shore he saw two other brothers, James and John, sitting in a boat with their father, Zebedee, mending their nets. And he called them to come, too. They immediately followed him, leaving the boat and their father behind" (Matt. 4:21-22, NLT).

Why God might have called David as a young adult

- ⬦ His whole life was in front of him.
  He would have years in his future to make an impact for God.

- ⬦ His faith and zeal were hot, unlike older generations.
  He was willing to attempt the impossible for God - not just the conventional.

- ⬦ He was teachable and available as a shepherd watching the sheep.
  He had time to worship and listen to God - and learn from Him as he waited.

- ⬦ He would give God all the glory since he was inexperienced.
  He knew he was young and inexperienced, so victory would belong to the Lord.

"Don't let anyone think less of you because you are young. Be an example to all believers in what you teach, in the way you live, in your love, your faithand your purity."

1 Timothy 4:12
(NLT)

Group Up

Reflect on ways that you think answering God's call on your life will change it.

Look at the great leaders of the Bible we have given as examples.

How were their lives impacted?

WHY SHOULD WE ANSWER GOD'S CALL?

So, even if God has called us to be leaders, why should we answer His call? Four reasons compel us to pick up the phone and answer God's call to become a leader.

Because Every Generation Must Reach Their Own Generation for Christ

Christianity is always one generation away from extinction. No one can reach our generation as effectively as we can. Each time God raises up a new generation of disciples, He commissions them to reach their own generation. We must become students of leadership because there's a world we must lead to Jesus.

Lessons from History

During the days of the apostle Paul, Asia Minor was the center for the Christian faith. It was the Bible belt of ancient times. Paul had planted churches all over that area. If we went there today, we would find present day Turkey - a hotbed for Islam. Why? The generations who followed Paul did not reach their own generation.

As late as three centuries ago, Europe was the center for Christianity. No longer. Europe is spiritually dry and decaying. Why? The generations who followed did not reach their own generation. How about our generation? It's our turn now!

Reflect and Respond...

We all have people that God places within our sphere of influence that we can best impact and reach. Who have you established a relationship with that God wants you to reach? How will you reach them?

Reflect

and

Respond

Because We Will Influence Others Whether We Want To or Not

Secondly, we must answer God's call because we have influence over others. Sociologists tell us the most introverted of people will influence 10,000 others in an average lifetime. Think about it. No matter how shy we are, we will rub off on 10,000 people before we die without even trying! And if we're a leader - even in little ways - how many might we influence? 50,000? 100,000?

On a scale of one to ten, we may never feel like a "ten" as a leader. Maybe we only feel like a "four". But don't you think we could grow from a "four" to a "seven" by studying leadership and becoming more effective as a leader? This is why we must study leadership. We must leverage our influence the best way possible for the King.

Trevor's Place

A boy named Trevor Ferrell founded Trevor's Place in Philadelphia, PA. At age 11, Trevor was watching the news when a story came on about the homeless in Philadelphia. He spoke to his parents that night and they agreed to pray about the need - but he knew that wasn't enough. He talked them into going downtown and giving a blanket and sack meal to a homeless person. That was just the beginning. Seventeen years later, Trevor's Place now employs several staff, has a location in the city and provides food and warmth to hundreds of homeless people in Philadelphia.

Because The World Needs Leaders Now More Than Ever

The third reason we must answer God's call is because the world needs leaders now more than ever. In recent times, many different leaders in varying leadership roles have failed.

Political	Business	Athletic	Church
Presidents and politicians have been indicted for immoral and illegal conduct while in office.	CEO's have a high rate of suicide because of the pressure to perform and the desire for more money.	Athletes have become primadonnas, often driven by money, fame, and drugs.	Televangelists, pastors, and other church leaders have fallen into sexual sin and financial irresponsibility.

Nothing is More Important

Just prior to the dawn of the 21st century, George Barna wrote: "After fifteen years of digging into the world around me, I have reached several conclusions regarding the future of the Christian church in America. The central conclusion is that the American church is dying due to lack of strong leadership. In this time of unprecedented opportunity and plentiful resources, the church is actually losing influence. The primary reason is the lack of leadership...Nothing is more important than leadership."[1]

> "In this time of unprecedented opportunity and plentiful resources, the church is actually losing influence. The primary reason is the lack of leadership...Nothing is more important than leadership."
> George Barna

Group Up

What is the consensus in your group?

Do you think that we are in need of leadership now more than ever?

Because When God Starts A Movement He Often Goes To Young People

The final reason we must become leaders is because God often starts movements with young people. Throughout the ages, God has raised up young people to accomplish what He could only do through their excitement, passion, and unquenchable spirit.

Young Leaders Who Impacted the World

⚙ Jesus' Disciples
Jesus' disciples were probably the same age as many of us. John was likely in his late teens when Jesus called him. He lived a long, full life. Jesus chose them because they would be willing to passionately follow Him and to try pulling off the impossible.

⚙ The Haystack Movement
The haystack movement began when college students were on their way to a church meeting one night. It began to rain, so they took cover under a haystack. When the thunderstorm grew worse, they decided to hold their own prayer meeting. Out of that meeting came a movement of missionaries that changed the world at that time.

⚙ The Cambridge Seven
Ever heard of the Cambridge Seven? Less than 150 years ago, in the 1860s, seven college students at Cambridge University in England decided to meet together to pray and discuss the needs of the world around them. They were especially burdened by China. From those seven students came a movement of workers that impacted China by the end of the 19th century.

⚙ The Student Volunteer Movement
At the end of the 19th century, Christians felt the same urgency that we did at the end of the 20th century. They wanted to finish the task of world evangelism. Men like John Mott and Dwight Moody traveled to college campuses compelling students to surrender their lives to the cause of the Great Commission. It was called the Student Volunteer Movement. Before the movement was over, more than 100,000 students stood up to be part of it by giving, praying and going. More than 30,000 actually went overseas and packed all their belongings in a pine box. They knew that they would likely die early, and this box would serve as their casket.

⚙ Operation Mobilization & George Verwer
George Verwer was 18 years old when God burdened him with the Great Commission. He knew he had to do something as a student at college Moody Bible Institute. He took a team of other students to Mexico to serve there and to enable his friends to catch a vision for the world - and that began the ministry we call Operation Mobilization today. Hundreds of thousands of people have been impacted by the tens of thousands of missionaries they have sent out. It all started with a student.

⚙ John Wesley
John Wesley began his "Holy Club" when he was only a teenager. By the age of 17 he founded the organization that become the Methodist Church.

⚙ George Williams
George Williams was 23 when he founded the Y.M.C.A.

Group Up

What is your reaction to the idea that God often starts a movement with young people?

Discuss as a group what your thoughts are on this.

☺ **Charles Spurgeon**
Charles Spurgeon was a well-known pulpit orator at 16. He was only 21 years old when he became pastor of the Metropolitan Chapel where he spoke to crowds of 10,000.

☺ **John Calvin**
John Calvin was just 17 when he entered the pastorate.

☺ **Bill Bright & Campus Crusade for Christ**
Bill Bright, who has been one of the most influential Christian leaders of our time, was a student being mentored by Henrietta Mears at Hollywood Presbyterian church. One night, he spent most of the night praying, feeling as though God was calling him to reach the UCLA campus. Miss Mears asked: "Why stop with just that campus? Why not the rest of the nation?" From that challenge, Campus Crusade for Christ (CCC) began, and at last count, CCC has reached one billion people for Christ around the world. Students have done most of the work!

MAKINGS OF A GREAT LEADER

A leader is many things and each person has a unique style. These men who were great Christian leaders throughout history had very different personalities and styles of leadership from each other. Let's take a look at some other great characteristics of leaders. Every great leader is a . . .

- Futurist – their dreams are bigger than their memories.
- Lobbyist – their causes outlive and out speak their critics.
- Catalyst – they initiate movement and momentum for others.
- Specialist – they don't try to do everything, but contribute in one area.
- Optimist – they believe in their cause and their people beyond reason.
- Economist – they marshal every resource as a sacrificial steward of the cause.
- Activist – they are "doers" and empower other people to unleash their potential.
- Strategist – they shrewdly plan how they can best harness and leverage their influence.
- Enthusiast – they have passion that defies logic and they magnetically attract others.
- Pragmatist – their legend is that they have solved practical problems people face.
- Industrialist – they are not afraid to roll up their sleeves and work long and hard.
- Finalist – they labor with diligence and devotion to the end; they finish well.

Reflect and Respond...

Which three roles are the easiest for you?

Which three are the hardest?

What will you do to develop the roles that don't come easily to you?

Reflect

and

Respond

Assess Yourself

This topic is easy to embrace in our minds but harder to grasp with our hearts. We can lead now! We don't have to wait to make a major impact on our world! After looking at how God has called young people throughout the ages to leadership, do you believe that God will use you to lead? What doubts, if any, do you have?

What specific habits for better leadership can you begin to cultivate? (For example, begin a personal growth plan by reading and listening to tapes, find a mentor, be more self-disciplined, change your attitude and speech, be a better time-manager, etc.) Can you jot down at least two?

1.

2.

What vision has God placed within your heart? Where can you begin to make an impact RIGHT NOW! (Through campus leadership, through a non-profit organization, through community involvement, through an entirely new venture, etc.) Write down your vision in a few words.

Commit to the Lord this plan of action. Ask Him to give you the strength to take the leap into greater levels of leadership. Once you've prayed, sign your name and the date below to seal your commitment.

Name: _____ Date: _____

Application

What is one step you will take as a result of this chapter? When will you take it? Who will hold you accountable? Review this chapter and think about what specifically you can do to take a step toward implementing the lessons in this session. Write out what you will do and when you will do it. Ask one person in the group to hold you accountable during the week. Be ready to share with the group next time you meet what step you took and anything you learned or gained from it.

Primary Colors of a Leader

FOUR ESSENTIAL QUALITIES WE NEED

The Four Essential Qualities of Effective Leaders

"No good tree bears bad fruit, nor does a bad tree bear good fruit. Each tree is recognized by its own fruit. People do not pick figs from thornbushes, or grapes from briers."
Luke 6:43-44

The Real Leader...

I heard a documentary about a very unlikely encounter between two Nebraska leaders. The first leader was Michael Weisser. Michael began to get involved in his community by asking neighbors what they thought the town needed. One common response had to do with the steadily growing ethnic population. African-Americans, Hispanics and Asians were moving into town, making both them and the locals uncomfortable. This sparked an idea for Mike. He began offering welcome baskets to these new neighbors. His idea was an instant success and a team assembled to help him with the project.

The second leader in this documentary was Larry Trapp, the local Grand Dragon of the Ku Klux Klan. Larry stood for everything contrary to what Michael was doing. In fact, he was also greeting new neighbors . . . he was seeking out these individuals and anonymously threatening their lives! Unhappy about Michael welcoming these same people, Larry promptly left a threatening message on his answering machine.

Since every call deserves a call back, Michael decided to leave Larry a voice message. "I got your phone call," he began, "and I just want you to know that I did a little homework on you too. I discovered that you are diabetic and confined to a wheelchair (both of these were true). I just thought that someone like you could use the help of someone like me. You see, I have a van and I'd be happy to pick you up and run some errands with you. If you ever could use my help, just let me know."

Michael left messages for four weeks, but never caught Larry at home. When they finally connected, Michael assured him that the offer was still good. Larry was dumfounded at first, yet he finally decided to take Michael up on the offer. For the next few weeks, the two men ran errands. One day, Larry finally asked Michael why he was helping him. Michael responded, "I'm trying to follow God as best I can. I'm just trying to do what I think God would do if He were here with you right now." Upon hearing this, Larry began to weep and shared his heart. Before the conversation was over, Larry was praying with Michael. His life would never be the same. And, neither would the life of the community where they lived.

The story was splashed across the morning papers: "KKK Leader Denounces the Klan." Larry not only quit the Klan, he publicly apologized to all the people he had threatened. He decided to join the basket ministry so he could personally take baskets to these people. He ended up moving in with Michael and was mentored by him for a year and a half before Larry died from his diabetic complications. By that time, the entire community had undergone a radical transformation, racially and spiritually. It all happened because one ordinary man decided to get involved and lead instead of playing it safe and minding his own business.

Basic Truth
All effective leaders possess four primary qualities: character, perspective, courage, and favor.

Guided Prayer
Lord, give me insight into what makes up a healthy, effective leader.

Make me sensitive to Your Spirit and show me the areas in which I need to grow and develop.

I desire to be transformed in my heart and mind so that I might reflect the qualities of a leader who is after Your own heart.

Amen.

True Leadership

Notice the authentic leadership in this story. No titles, positions or power was involved – only true leadership. Several observations may be made through the example of Michael Weisser.

True leadership . . .
- Does not depend upon conferred authority, titles, positions or fame.
- Can occur whenever a need emerges that sparks passion within someone.
- May take on a variety of methods, styles and appearances because the outcome is what is most important to the leader.
- Works toward a breakthrough of impact or achievement.
- Occurs when one person acts upon the vision of a preferred future and then mobilizes others to join in the cause.

Group Up

As a group, discuss what authentic leadership looks like.

Reflect and Respond...

What comes to mind when you hear the word leader? List six characteristics that make a good leader.

1.
2.
3.
4.
5.
6.

Reflect and Respond

Leadership is influence, nothing more, nothing less.

Leadership is Influence

Even if we do not "feel" like leaders, we must realize that leadership can be summed up in one simple word: **INFLUENCE**. Leadership is influence, nothing more, nothing less. And influence is something that every person has. Sociologists tell us that even the most introverted person will influence 10,000 people in his or her lifetime! If we are intentional about being leaders, think how many more people we will influence!

THE COMMON THREADS OF GREAT LEADERS

Three actions they take:	Three atmospheres they make:
THEY CAST VISION: Leaders possess and communicate a picture of their goals to others.	A SENSE OF DESTINY: Leaders have a picture of what they want and feel destined to fulfill it.
THEY IMPLEMENT STRATEGY: Leaders understand and implement steps toward reaching the goals.	A SENSE OF FAMILY: Leaders promote an atmosphere of support and belonging; no one feels alone in the task.
THEY EMPOWER PEOPLE: Leaders mobilize and equip people to join them in the cause.	A TENACIOUS SPIRIT: Leaders possess a resolve to reach the goal, whatever the cost or sacrifice.

Reflect and Respond...

As a leader, which of the three actions you have just read about, do you do most naturally? Are you a natural at casting vision, implementing strategy, or empowering people? Which do you struggle with?

Reflect

Which of the atmospheres do you create most easily when you lead? Do you have a strong sense of family, of destiny, or a tenacious spirit? With which do you struggle?

and

Respond

The Leadership Equation

The greatest masterpieces in the world all began with a few primary colors. I remember when my art history professor in college brought in several beautiful paintings. He described the unique details of each masterpiece. Afterward, however, he reminded us, "All of these began with just four primary colors: red, yellow, blue, and white."

This is a beautiful analogy. Like those paintings, you are a unique masterpiece. However, regardless of how unique you are, if you are to practice healthy, effective leadership, you will need to possess some common characteristics other leaders have as well. Just as an artist begins with a few basic colors, there are basic "colors" that make up every healthy, effective leader. Let's begin by looking at the primary colors of leadership.

The Primary Color

Healthy, effective, leadership results from "mixing" the following:

Character	Perspective	Courage	Favor
1. The leader's backbone	1. The leader's mind	1. The leader's will	1. The leader's heart
2. Discipline and responsibility	2. Vision and planning	2. Commitment and risk	2. People skills and charisma
3. Inward strength	3. Inward sight	3. Inward spirit	3. Inward savvy
4. An ability to stand up	4. An ability to see ahead	4. An ability to step out	4. An ability to soar above
THIS IS OUR INFRASTRUCTURE	THIS IS OUR INSIGHT	THIS IS OUR INITIATIVE	THIS IS OUR INFLUENCE

Character — Primary Color #1

Enables a leader to do what is right . . . even when it is difficult.

Character

The first primary color of leadership is character. Character is the foundation on which a leader's life is built. It all begins with character because leadership operates on the basis of trust. J.R. Miller said it well: "The only thing that walks back from the tomb with the mourners and refuses to be buried is the character of a man. What a man is survives him. It can't be buried." Character works for a leader in four essential ways:

Character . . .

- communicates credibility
- earns trust
- harnesses respect
- creates consistency

Reflect and Respond...

Think of a leader you admire. How does his or her character communicate credibility, harness respect, create consistency, and earn trust?

Reflect

and

Respond

REQUIRED INGREDIENTS FOR CHARACTER

In order to be a person of character, the following ingredients need to be in place:
- Development of personal disciplines
- Development of personal security and identity
- Development of personal convictions, values and ethics

Real Life...

In the early days of American history, several men wanted to become president. One of these men was Aaron Burr. . . yet it was in his early days that he actually ruined his chance of becoming president. One day, he stepped up to address the congress and to present a bill that was very unpopular. A friend grabbed his coat, pulled him aside, and whispered passionately, "If you speak on behalf of this piece of legislation you will kill your chance to become president!" Aaron Burr simply looked down at the paper in his hand and asked, "But is this bill right?" After a moment of thought, his friend responded, "Well, yes, I believe it is." Aaron Burr then spoke the classic words: "Well, then I would rather be right than be president."

Group Up

Share who you came up with as examples of leaders who are people of character.

Talk about the ways in which they demonstrate that.

Steps for Developing Character

Solid character does not just happen – it must be purposely developed. Below are six proven steps for developing fracture-resistant character. You can begin these now!

- Discipline yourself to do two things you don't like to do every week.
- Fix your eyes on a clear, specific purpose.
- Investigate the "whys" behind God's commands.
- Interview a leader who has integrity: How did they build it into their life?
- Adjust and monitor your motives for why you do what you do.
- Write out the promises you've made. Take responsibility for all your actions and emotions.

Reflect and Respond...

How would you rate yourself on the character scale? For example:

◇ When you say you'll finish an assignment, do you always follow through?

◇ Do you only claim credit for work that you personally have done?

◇ Do you color situations to reflect how you want them to appear?

On a scale of 1 to 10 (ten being the highest), how solidly would you rate your character?

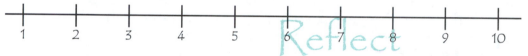

1   2   3   4   5   6   7   8   9   10

Explain the rating you chose and evaluate what is keeping you from having a perfect "10" character.

Look at the list at the top of this page titled "Steps for Developing Character." Which of those things can you make a part of your life as you strive to improve your character? How will you implement those steps?

Perspective — Primary Color #2

Enables a leader to see and understand what must happen to reach the target.

Perspective

The second primary color for healthy, effective leadership is perspective. Jesus began His training of the twelve by working on their perspective. He worked on their vision and how they saw life. He knew if He could get them to *think* differently, He could get them to *act* differently.

Character is essential, but anyone can have good character. Perspective is the first quality that separates leaders from followers. Leaders think differently than followers. They envision differently than followers. They see *beyond*, they see *bigger*, and they see *before* followers do. Dr. Robert Clinton said: "The primary difference between a follower and a leader is perspective. The primary difference between a leader and an effective leader is better perspective."

Leaders see the big picture and the little process . . .

1. They first choose their Vision. What is the goal?

2. They then choose their Venue. What is the strategy to reach it?

3. Finally, they choose their Vehicles. What are the systems needed to move ahead?

Real Life

In 1982 a theme park was finished. It was a marvelous park, and the date was set for the grand opening. The owner of the park had already passed away. The park executives asked his wife to cut the ribbon and say a few words. When the Master of Ceremonies called her up to the podium, he smiled and said, "I just wish your husband could have seen this!" She smiled and responded by saying, "He did."

The original creator had "seen" the park inside of himself long before everyone else saw it in real life. This is what attracts people to leaders. Leaders seem to have a clear picture of a goal and they know the steps necessary to reach it. This is attractive to others because God designed everyone to operate off of the power of vision. Vision and purpose give people energy. The clearer the vision is, the more motivating it can become. If you have a goal that is both clear and relevant, others will eventually become interested.

When Dr. Martin Luther King stood on the steps of the Lincoln Memorial in Washington D.C., he communicated his vision to the world. It became the most famous speech of the 20th century: "I have a dream..." He described it in great detail over and over... and it began to capture the hearts and imaginations of millions.

REQUIRED INGREDIENTS FOR PERSPECTIVE

A leader who possesses perspective is able to do the following:
• Build and cast vision
• Plan and prepare the strategy to fulfill the vision
• Discern the process and people needed to reach the goal

"The primary difference between a follower and a leader is perspective. The primary difference between a leader and an effective leader is better perspective."

Dr. Robert Clinton

Steps for Developing Perspective

Anyone can develop perspective in their life if they choose to think differently. Below are six steps to help us enhance our perspective.

- Watch the news or read the newspaper and ask: What could be done to solve these problems? Choose a crisis and list solution steps you would take if you were in charge.
- Groom the optimist in you. Read and listen to positive books and tapes. Feed yourself with big ideas from great people.
- Write out your dreams. What would you attempt to do if you did not fear failure?
- Interview a visionary leader. How do they think? How do they perceive things?
- Identify one burden you've embraced. Set some goals to address it.
- Post photos, pictures and quotes that represent your goals and dreams in your room.

Reflect and Respond...

In the space provided, write about a vision that you have for your personal life. What venue and vehicles will you choose to make your vision a reality? Discuss the goal, strategy, and systems.

Reflect

and

Respond

List three things you will do this week to improve your perspective as a leader.

Group Up

Share with the group some of the solutions you came up with to address the needs in this world or on your campus.

When you look at the needs around you on your campus or in your world, do you get any ideas for solutions to those needs? What idea do you have that could be the "seed" for a God-given vision in the future?

Courage — Primary Color #3

Enables a leader to initiate and take the risk to step out toward a goal.

With only character and perspective, a leader may still lack action. Someone once said, "There is nothing more common in America than people with great ideas that do nothing about them." This is why we need to develop courage. Only courage enables a leader to step out and implement the vision they possess inside of themselves. The only measure of what we believe is what we do. To know what people believe, don't read what they write, don't ask what they think, just observe what they do. Our personal lives shrink or expand in proportion to our courage.

Courage is...

- contagious
- vision in action
- the power to let go of the familiar
- risking and seizing what is essential for growth
- initiating and doing what you are afraid of doing

Real Life

My first big lesson in courage came when I was in college. On an episode of 20/20, I saw the four members of the heavy metal band, KISS. They boasted about the drugs, sex and money they had, laughing about their exploits in front of millions of teenagers. At that point, I prayed: "God, somebody ought to do something about them!" Suddenly, I felt the Holy Spirit prodding me. In fact, I sensed He was impressing me to go and share Jesus with the members of KISS! The idea scared me to death, but the more I tried to ignore it, the deeper the impression became.

The next fall KISS came to town and God opened up a door for me to talk to them. I found the hotel where they were staying and talked to a maid about which room they were in. I spotted their bodyguard outside their door at midnight. When I asked if I could talk to Gene Simmons and the rest of KISS, he reminded me he was there to protect them from people like me. Then I showed him my personal tracts I had created for the band. I asked him if he would simply give them to the guys and I would leave. He took the tracts, then suggested I wait around a while. He told me that after the concerts, the band usually visited the bar and had a little nightcap – at about 2:00 am. If I was willing to wait, I could talk to them then.

I did wait, but not without a major battle with fear. I saw visions of worst-case-scenarios: getting cussed at, beat up, and thrown out of the bar by those guys. Fortunately, I sat down, prayed, and God reminded me of why I was there. I ended up meeting all the members of KISS and shared Christ with each one of them that night. My greatest take-away, however, was simply learning how much God wants to use ordinary people to do extraordinary ministry...if they can only get beyond their fears.

Reflect and Respond...

Do you consider yourself a courageous person? Write about the last time that you did something that required great courage. If possible, jot down two things you can do to develop courage.

1.

2.

REQUIRED INGREDIENTS FOR COURAGE

Being a person of courage includes:

⬦ Making and keeping commitments

⬦ Building the capacity to take risks

⬦ Lobbying for a breakthrough in a cause

Steps for Developing Courage

To improve your courage, do the following . . .

- Attempt something each week that you could not possibly pull off without God.
- Invite accountability regarding commitments and decisions you've made.
- Give an all-out commitment to a good habit for a set time.
- Interview a courageous person. What gives them their courage?
- Do the thing you fear the most and the death of fear will be certain.
- Force yourself to be a decision-maker and a responsibility-taker.

Group Up

As a group, recall past leadership situations when you needed courage.

Also discuss future leadership roles that may require courage.

Reflect and Respond...

How do you tend to handle fear? Do you embrace it?

Are stretching experiences a regular part of your life? Reflect

and

Or have you retreated so far into your comfort zone that you don't ever feel fear? Respond

Write about a time in your life or leadership experience when you lacked courage.

In what area of your life do you need courage right now? How can you develop courage in that specific area?

Favor — Primary Color #4

Enables a leader to attract and empower others to join them in the cause.

Finally, a leader must display relational skills to mobilize people. Without favor, a person may reach a goal, but fail to take anyone along with them. Leaders, by definition, always have followers.

If we have character, perspective and courage, we will likely become an entrepreneur who attempts great things in our life. However, we may be acting alone. The entrepreneur often travels alone. Leaders always take others with them.

Key elements...
- **Communication** – Leaders must develop listening skills and the ability to share ideas convincingly.
- **Motivation** – Leaders must mobilize others for mutual benefit and empowerment.
- **Delegation** – Leaders must share their authority, responsibility and ownership of the vision.
- **Confrontation** – Leaders must have backbone and be able to resolve relational differences.
- **Reproduction** – Leaders must be able to equip and train a team of people to accomplish the goal.

Reflect and Respond...

Which of the "key elements" of favor come easily to you? Which are the most difficult for you? Why? Write them under the appropriate heading for you.

Easily	Difficult

Real Life

When John Maxwell became the pastor of Skyline Church in 1981, he faced a formidable challenge. He followed the founding pastor, Dr. Orval Butcher, who had led the church for 27 years. Consequently, some of the congregation didn't like John Maxwell. He was replacing their hero. Several people displayed their displeasure during John's first year, particularly one man, Harry Mitchell. He wouldn't even talk to John. Fortunately, John had developed some marvelous people skills and decided he would love Harry until he responded to his leadership. He asked Harry to meet him for a special one-to-one appointment. When the two sat down, John simply asked Harry to tell him a bit about Dr. Butcher. Harry lit up. With great enthusiasm he shared for 45 minutes about what a great leader Pastor Butcher was. (John had succeeded in getting him to talk!) After Harry finished, John smiled and said, "Harry, you're right. Pastor Butcher really is a great leader. I want you to know that I think you should continue loving him just the way you do right now." Then John paused. "But Harry, I have a question for you. After you love Dr. Butcher with all that love, if there is any love left over — could I have that?" Harry began to cry. He knew the game he had been playing. That day Harry hugged his new pastor for the first time. From that time on, every Sunday, Harry would initiate a hug with his new pastor. Each time Harry would hug Pastor Maxwell he would whisper in his ear, "This is the love I got left over."

REQUIRED INGREDIENTS FOR FAVOR

To be a leader who gains favor, you must focus on...
- ◇ Building people skills
- ◇ Building personal charisma
- ◇ Communication, motivation, delegation, confrontation, & reproduction

Word Pictures

One of the ways to develop favor is by learning to connect with others. Four different word pictures exemplify how we are to relate to others in conversation. Put yourself in the following roles and you will build favor.

The Host
Good hosts always take initiative and see to it that their guests are comfortable. We are to host the conversations and relationships of our lives.

Think about how a host takes initiative and makes you feel welcome in his/her home?

The Doctor
Doctors never give a prescription before first diagnosing the person. An accurate diagnosis requires asking questions and conducting an examination. We are to poke and prod with questions that inquire about others' interests. We are to be a "relational doctor".

Examine how you can inquire inductively about others' interests with questions?

The Counselor
The mark of a good counselor is active listening. Good counselors earn their right to speak by listening. We, too, must be active listeners, validating the other person.

How often do you take a break in your schedule to really listen to others?

The Tour Guide
A tour guide is not hired to fellowship or to be a buddy, but to get the people to their desired destination. We are to lead others through a process and get them to a destination.

How does a tour guide lead you on a journey? (Hint: the difference between a travel agent and a tour guide is that one of them goes with you!)

Role Play

If you are in a group, divide up into pairs. Assign each pair one of the four word pictures: the host, the doctor, the counselor, and the tour guide. In the context of a leadership situation, have one person play the assigned role and have the other respond to the role their partner is playing. Demonstrate the role in your conversation. What can you say to become an effective host, doctor, counselor, and tour guide as a leader? Debrief your experience. Discuss what each person playing the role could do to better connect and serve as a leader in these various roles.

Steps for Developing Favor

Just like trade skills can be learned, our people skills can also be developed. But, unless our heart genuinely loves people, our skills can't effectively be developed. Without love, the result of this development will be manipulation, not favor. However, once our heart is right, our skills can greatly enhance our leadership.

• Learn to "host" the relationships and conversations you engage in.
• Determine to be other-centered, focusing on other's needs, not on yours.
• Become a "good finder." Find one good quality in others and affirm it.
• Make deposits in the lives of people (encouragement, good books, contacts, etc.).
• Identify the strengths in people and help them find a place to employ those strengths.
• Interview a people-person. How did they develop their charisma?

Reflect and Respond...

Are you already playing the role of the host, doctor, counselor, or tour guide in any of your relationships? In what ways?

Reflect

and

What will be most difficult for you as you serve in these various roles?

Respond

What Happens if I'm Missing a Quality?

Now that we've looked at different leadership qualities, let's look at what happens when one of these qualities is missing. In reality, it is unlikely that we have conquered each of these areas in our personal lives. It's important to recognize where our weaknesses are so we can work on their improvement.

Over the long haul, a leader must have all four qualities in order to perform at an optimal level. We see this truth verified in the lives of those we read about in the pages of Scripture. Notice what happens when just one component is missing from the equation.

perspective + courage + favor – character = SAMSON

Read Judges 13:24-16:31. Samson failed miserably because he didn't develop character. He knew right from wrong, possessed courage, and at times held favor and influence. But Samson never mastered character. He had strong biceps, but a weak backbone.

character + perspective + favor – courage = PILATE

Read John 18:28-19:16. Even if he possessed character, Pilate failed miserably. He may have had the right perspective and the power, but he failed to do what was right and brave due to his lack of courage. He wouldn't take responsibility for the trial of Jesus, but rather washed his hands of it. Good leaders don't shirk responsibility.

character + courage + favor – perspective = SIMON PETER

Read Matthew 16:21-23. Peter displayed character and courage numerous times during Jesus' ministry and he seemed to have favor with his colleagues. But gaps in his perspective were clearly experienced. Sometimes Jesus even had to correct him in public!

character + perspective + courage - favor = JOSHUA & CALEB

Read Numbers 13:17-33. Caleb and Joshua came back from spying out the land with great perspective and courage, but they did not have enough favor to influence the people to move forward. Because they didn't have favor with the people, that generation was never permitted to make it into the Promised Land.

Reflect and Respond...

All of us have different areas of strength and weakness. Which of these biblical characters do you identify with the most?

Group Up

Can your group come up with any other leaders who were missing one of the four qualities?

What was the result in their leadership and organization?

Reflect

and

Respond

Toxic Leaders

By reflecting on past leaders we can see leadership strengths and weaknesses. If we realize the mistakes of other leaders, we can learn from them and avoid those same mistakes.

Leaders like Nero, Adolf Hitler and Joseph Stalin were destined to sabotage themselves. Nero possessed an enlarged ego that choked out his perspective. Hitler's lack of character choked out his perspective and favor. Stalin's character was so absent that he lost all favor with people and never got it back. These leaders' impact ended up being negative and short lived. They did not possess all the qualities of whole and healthy leaders. Toxic leaders often sabotage themselves for several reasons.

Toxic leaders tend to sabotage themselves because they have . . .
- Too much ego
- Too much control
- Too much insecurity
- Too little character
- Too little charisma
- Too little servanthood

Assess Yourself...

Review the four primary colors of effective, healthy leadership. Do you exhibit these qualities in your life and leadership? As a leader, which of the four qualities are you strongest in? In which are you the weakest?

Looking back at the steps for developing the different qualities of healthy leadership, write down specifically what you will do to enhance the quality that needs developing in your life.

Application

What is one step you will take as a result of this chapter? When will you take it? Who will hold you accountable? Review this chapter and think about what specifically you can do to take a step toward implementing the lessons in this session. Write out what you will do and when you will do it. Ask one person in the group to hold you accountable during the week. Be ready to share with the group next time you meet what step you took and anything you learned or gained from it.

Becoming a Person of Influence

HOW GOD BUILDS A PERSON INTO A LEADER

"I write to you, dear children, because your sins have been forgiven on account of his name. I write to you, fathers, because you have known him who is from the beginning. I write to you, young men, because you have overcome the evil one."
1 John 2:12-13

Inward Surgery

It was 1921 when Dr. Evan Kane first proposed the idea of doing surgery on someone using only local anesthesia. Up until then, doctors had always put patients to sleep, knocking them out for hours afterward. He wanted to do it with the patient wide awake. His New York hospital approved of it, but only if he could find his own patient. He went to work on finding a patient and date to perform this historic surgery. On February 15, it all happened. Meticulously, he removed the appendix from the patient. When he sewed the skin back up, it was such a success that all on-lookers broke out into applause. It was one for the record books. Here's the irony. The surgeon that day in 1921, was Dr. Evan Kane, and the patient… was also Dr. Evan Kane. That day he did surgery on himself!

As we grow into spiritual leaders, some inward surgery will have to be done. I believe that no one can do it for us. We must choose to take out those things that hinder our growth and cooperate with God's pruning process. This story illustrates precisely what I want to accomplish here. This session will provide you with the scalpel and the scissors for you to do the necessary surgery on your life as you become a person of influence.

The Big Picture

There's another analogy that illustrates what I want to accomplish. An eight-year old boy was trying to watch a parade by peering through a knothole in a fence. He could only see whatever came along directly in front of him: first a clown, then the band, next came a float. At one point, his dad came behind him and hoisted him upon his shoulders high above the fence. For the first time, he could see the panorama of the entire parade!

That is the purpose of this lesson. It is designed to lift us up above our lives and to give us an overview of the journey God desires to take us on throughout our lifetime. We will examine God's objectives in each phase of our development as well as our appropriate responses to those phases. Why is this important for us to understand? Because if we can see the big picture of what God is trying to accomplish, we can begin to cooperate with God in the surgical process. Let's fasten our seat belts . . . we're about to see the big picture of the incredible adventure awaiting us!

How God Builds a Person into a Leader

Basic Truth
If we see the big picture of what God is trying to accomplish in our lives, we can better cooperate with God in the process.

Guided Prayer
Lord Jesus,
I know there is major surgery that needs to be done on my heart and in my life.

Expose the areas of weakness and sin in my life, and rid me of all that would hinder my growth and Your will for my life.

I desire nothing more than to grow into the fullness of who You desire me to be in Christ.

Amen.

One Step at a Time...

We all wish maturity would come instantly – but that's not realistic. Before we look at the phases, let's look at some passages that illustrate the idea of progressive growth.

Read 1 John 2:12-14, our key verse for this section. In this text, John speaks to three different groups of people, who represent three stages of spiritual maturity. Notice that each group (fathers, young men, and children) all face different issues in their life.

What does this passage teach you about God's view of growth?

Also Read:
- Matthew 25:21
- Jeremiah 12:5
- 1 Peter 2:2
- Hebrews 5:12-6:3
- Colossians 2:6-7
- 1 Corinthians 3:1-3

Jot down some words or phrases to describe what these passages say about spiritual growth.

- Matthew 25:21:

- 1 Peter 2:2:

- Colossians 2:6-7:

- Jeremiah 12:5:

- Hebrews 5:12-6:3:

- 1 Corinthians 3:1-3:

Group Up

Discuss your reflections on 1 John 2:12-14 with your group.

Do you find the idea of progressive growth encouraging or discouraging?

How can you as a fellowship of believers encourage one another in this process of growth?

THE SIX PHASES OF OUR GROWTH

Growth comes in many different forms and often it feels like there's no rhyme or reason to it. But, we can recognize certain landmarks along the way. This lesson will put our lives in the form of six phases – from birth to death – but the rate at which we go through these phases will differ for each individual. As we work through these phases, think about where you have been, where you are, and where you want to be. It's time to look over the fence and see the big picture!

Phase One: Providential Beginnings

This stage generally covers our lives from birth up to conversion. It includes all the things that happen before we get together with God. Isn't it great to know that He develops us even in the times of life before we are cooperating with Him? God is completely providential and sovereign. He is already preparing us to be used by Him.

Phase One
Providential
Beginnings

God's Objectives for Phase One...

⊚ **Personality Development** – God desires our unique development (temperament, talents, preferences, style, character).

⊚ **Testimony Development** – God is shaping a story of His grace. He uses everything – the good and the bad.

⊚ **Teachability** – We must each recognize the need for His control. Our world today sends messages demanding that we be "in control" at all times. It usually takes deliberate thought and action to surrender ourselves to God's control.

⊚ **Basic Ethics** – God wants to build in us an awareness of right and wrong. We begin to think like He thinks.

⊚ **Healthy Emotions** – God desires to construct in us a positive mental and emotional framework.

⊚ **Positive Attitude** – We are to build an optimistic perspective on our life and our future. This perspective will be optimal for what He wants to do later.

The Construction of a Life...

Your life can be compared to the building of a house. Phase One is like the foundation of the house. The foundation that every home is built upon may appear dull prior to the walls being constructed. Have you ever driven through a new neighborhood when all you could see was a foundation and a few pipes sticking up from the ground? Not very exciting. However, that foundation is the most critical ingredient to the endurance of the structure. The same is true with our lives. Phase One may seem uneventful and unglamorous, but it's the foundation upon which the rest of your life is built!

Reflect and Respond...

What is unique about you? What attributes exist inside you that make you different?

Reflect
and
Respond

You made all the delicate, inner parts of my body and knit me together in my mothers' womb. Thank you for making me so wonderfully complex! Your workmanship is marvelous – and how well I know it. You watched me as I was being formed in utter seclusion, as I was woven together in the dark of the womb. You saw me before I was born. Every day of my life was recorded in your book. Every moment was laid out before a single day had passed."
Psalm 139:13-16
(NLT)

Group Up
Take some time to share your faith stories in the group.

How has God uniquely fashioned each of you and your life story?

⋄ Have a positive attitude and perspective toward all circumstances, realizing that God is preparing you for something.

⋄ Take advantage of the lessons God teaches at this foundational stage!

Phase Two: Character & Spiritual Formation

Once we pass through Providential Beginnings, Phase Two begins. It optimally begins at our conversion. For the first time, we can choose to cooperate with God's purposes for us. His purpose is to develop our spirit and our character. His focus is on our private, personal disciplines, not so much the development of our talents or skills. We tend to by-pass these character builders because they bring us no immediate fan-fare or glamour, no spotlights or microphones. Motivation can be tough because it often must come from within. Few people from our places of employment evaluate our quiet time with God and we will never be promoted based on our Scripture memory or intimacy with God. Most people (even leaders) find it difficult to consistently focus on these disciplines.

Our temptation is to take short cuts on our character development. We want to hurry through this stage of our life. We yearn to move on to outward skills and charisma; the things that others see and applaud. After all, what's the big deal about our character?

Short Changing Yourself

A millionaire contracted a builder to construct a house for him. The budget was $400,000 and the builder was told to keep any money left over from the project. Because he wanted to make as much money for himself as he could, the builder scrimped on everything possible in every part of the house. Taking many short cuts, he built the house as fast as he could. When he finally got done, he went back to the millionaire and said, "The house is done, here are the keys!" The millionaire smiled, pushed the keys back into the man's hands and stated, "Oh, I forgot to tell you. The house is yours."

The builder had the chance to create a mansion for himself, yet he chose to build a flimsy shack, not knowing he was cheating himself. Overlooking our character development results in a similar surprise. God hands over our lives to us and lets us do with it as we like. When we cut corners on the important basics, we are like the builder. We think we are getting away with something when we do just enough to be a good person, but ignore the solid formation of our spirit and character. We'll never accomplish anything great for Him without building an infrastructure of discipline and character. Great character supports great conduct.

God's Objectives for Phase Two...

☺ **Intimacy** - God desires a close relational experience with us, not just a cognitive, academic understanding of Him. Read John 15:9 and John 17:3.

☺ **Discernment** - God wants us to develop the ability to distinguish between right and wrong. We begin to think like God thinks, and value what He values. Read 1 Corinthians 2:14-16.

- **Lordship** – God wants an obedient heart. He desires us to obey out of love for Him, not out of duty or performance. This means settling the Lordship issue: God calls the shots, we don't. Read Matthew 7:21 and Luke 6:46.

- **Security** – We must develop a deep inner life. This means our emotional security is cemented in the truth of Scripture, not in the approval of others. If we start serving without a sense of personal security, we will eventually sabotage ourselves. Read Galatians 6:3–5.

- **Identity** – God desires us to possess a healthy self-image and self-esteem where our identity is established in who He says we are. Identity and security are virtually inseparable. If we don't get our identity settled, the pressures of leadership will surely shape us into someone we never intended to become. Read 2 Corinthians 5:16-18.

- **Values & Personal Disciplines** – We must develop disciplines like Bible study, prayer, and fasting, as well as values by which to live. These enable us to delay gratification and live on purpose. They also strengthen the infrastructure of our lives so we can stand when the heat is on. God knows how foundational these objectives are to the health and vitality of our lives. Without them in place, we would not make it very far without problems! Read 1 Corinthians 9:24–27.

Group Up

Share with the group which objective(s) in Phase Two you struggle with the most and why?

Talk as a group about what can be done to grow stronger in these areas.

Neglecting personal disciplines makes us like a house with termites. . . . We look great on the outside, but we are crumbling on the inside.

Reflect and Respond...

Review God's objectives in this phase. Which areas are the strongest in your life right now? Are there objectives you can share with another person? Make a commitment to do this ASAP.

Reflect

Which areas are weakest in your life right now?

and

Respond

What disciplines do you need to build into your life right now?

"Being" before "Doing"

What I Am	What I Do	Result
Humble	Rely on God	God's Power
Convictional	Do what's right	Trust and commitment
Visionary	Set Goals	High Morale & Excitement

This diagram was developed by Dr. John Maxwell. In it he illustrates the need to move from the left column (What I Am) toward the right column (Result) via the middle column (What I Do). But, because we are so preoccupied with results, performance, and production, we're often tempted to move from right to left. We need to focus on "being" before "doing" if we are ever going to achieve permanent results.

For instance, we may be so consumed with desiring to see power in our lives (Result), that we move toward the left and try feverishly to rely on God since that's what produces a powerful life. Most of the time our attempts are done in our own strength and are short-lived. We become frustrated.

What God is saying to us, however, is, "Why don't you simply become humble? Why not develop humility in your 'being' - then you will naturally rely on me, and it will result in receiving My power." Jesus taught that a good tree naturally bears good fruit.

Reflect and Respond...

Do you see patterns of "doing" before "being" in your own life? What things can you do to reverse your focus?

Reflect

and

Why is it difficult for you to address these Phase Two issues?

Respond

YOUR PART...

- Become involved in some form of ministry or service. Spiritual muscles are exercised by serving!
- Be faithful and consistent in your personal spiritual disciplines.
- Meditate regularly on the Word. Know it and derive your self-image from it.
- Ask God to break you and shape you.

Group Up

Discuss ways to "be" before you "do."

What can you come up with as a group?

Phase Three: Service & Application

By Phase Three, it's time to leave the bench and start working! In the early stages of our Christian life, most of our growth comes from listening to instruction. By this phase, God draws a line in the sand and states, "You've got to get up and do something about what you know, or you will stunt your growth." In Phase Three, the primary means of growth is action. It comes from applying what you know. Now you're prepared to balance nutrition (milk) with exercise (meat).

How We Grow and Mature...

Read Hebrews 5:12-6:3. The text talks about two kinds of Christians: babies and mature adults. It speaks of two kinds of food: milk and meat (solid food). Notice that the items we would list under the "milk" category are primarily instructional in nature, (6:1-2). The items we would list under the "meat" category are application in nature, (5:14). In other words, contrary to modern belief, "meat" is not simply deeper teaching or preaching on Sunday morning. It is obedience. It is practicing the "milk." Even Jesus said that His "food" is to "do the will of him who sent me" (John 4:34).

Babies	Mature
"milk"	"meat"
Instruction (Hebrews 6:1-2)	Application (Hebrews 5:14)

" 'My food,' said Jesus, 'is to do the will of him who sent me and to finish his work.' "
John 4:34

Reflect and Respond...

What does this say to us about God's view of maturity?

What does it say about Phase Three in our leadership growth?

Group Up

Discuss as a group
this idea that as we
move up in leadership,
we lose our rights.

How did Paul
understand this?
Refer to 1 Corinthian
9:19-20,22-23.

God's Objectives for Phase Three...

☉ **Submission** – God desires our submission and our loyalty to authority, even when we disagree with those in charge. We won't be good leaders unless we first learn to be good followers. If we don't learn to listen and submit now, how will we do it when we are the leader? Read Romans 13:1-7.

☉ **Vision and Purpose** – God desires to develop in us a burden and a vision, in that order. Our life purpose is often revealed as we develop these, and experiment with different types of ministry. When we begin to see where our passions lie, our purpose becomes much clearer. Read Philippians 3:7-14.

☉ **Discovery & Use of Gifts** – Optimally, in this phase, we locate our spiritual gift-mix, and begin to identify our primary motivational gift (Rom. 12). This gift is the central "hub", around which our other gifts will revolve. We begin to understand who we are and who we are not; our strengths and weaknesses. Read Romans 12:6-8 & 1 Peter 4:10.

☉ **Responsibility** – Here we must recognize that to make things happen, we are responsible to initiate action. We cannot sit around waiting for a wise mentor or a perfect service opportunity to come our way. We've got to assume responsibility for our lives and go after what we know will help us grow. Read Galatians 6:4-9.

☉ **Sacrifice** – We must become willing to give up rights and relationships in order to grow. To get us where God wants to us to go, He teaches us that we must surrender the things that may be hindering our growth. This may mean giving up a dating relationship or a friendship, or a habit that we have. At this point, we surrender our lives to a "giving mode" rather than a "receiving mode." Read 1 Corinthians 9:19-23.

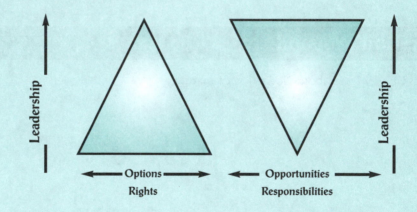

As we move up in leadership, the amount of responsibility and sacrifice in our life must increase. When first coming to Christ we have the widest amount of options (the base of the triangle). But as we move upward in our leadership and ministry, those options narrow. Unlike the world around us, leadership means giving up options, not gaining them (Matt. 20:25-27). Our goal is to reach the pinnacle of that triangle where we can declare with the apostle Paul, "I am a bond-servant of Jesus Christ."

☉ **People Skills & a Shepherd's Heart** – God desires that we become a lover of people and that we develop people skills and discernment in relationships. Even before we master techniques for ministry, we are to develop a deep compassion for others that moves us to action. Read 1 Peter 4:8 & 1 Corinthians 13.

Real Life...

Hoping to share his faith in Christ, a friend of mine named Eric gave a tract to a man on the street. He had no idea this man was an atheist. The man's anger toward God became evident as he ripped up the tract and hissed profanity at Eric. Ironically, instead of retaliating in defense, tears welled up in Eric's eyes. He didn't say a word. He just stood there on the sidewalk, crying. When the atheist looked up and finally saw his tears, he was stunned. After an awkward pause, the atheist quietly stooped down to pick up his litter, stuffed the ripped pages in his pocket and walked away.

A few days later Eric's phone rang. It was the stranger he had met on the street. The man explained that after taping the tract back together, he discovered Eric's number on the back and wanted to let him know that he had read it through twice and prayed "that little prayer" at the end to invite Christ to take over his life. He'd been transformed.

Eric was dumfounded. He didn't know what to say except, "Why?" The man answered, "I've never seen anyone truly care about whether I got it or not. I thought Christians were just angry, narrow people going through the motions. But, for the first time, I saw someone who really cared about me and I figured I ought to read what you had to say."

It was a shepherd's heart, not eloquence that was needed in this situation. It took a vessel of genuine compassion to get the truth through to the unbeliever standing in front of him. God refines our hearts, getting the inner qualities in place so that we are able to do the same.

Group Up

Which objective(s) in Phase Three do you find difficult?

Which have you taken on without a problem?

Share your thoughts with the group.

The Construction of a Life...

If we were to continue our "house" analogy, Phase Three represents all of the functional dimensions of the house: the plumbing, the electricity, the heating and air conditioning, and other items that make it work. It's now livable and functional.

Reflect and Respond...

Are you anywhere near this phase in your own life? How much "milk" and "meat" do you partake of in your life right now? Do you practice what you know?

Reflect

and

Can you spot something hindering your growth right now? What is keeping you from giving it up?

Respond

- Become strictly accountable to a ministry position.
- Work to develop relationships.
- Experiment with your spiritual gift-mix to understand your strengths and weaknesses.
- Become a strategic prayer warrior.
- Master time management – make a "time budget" to redeem time instead of wasting it.
- Share your faith regularly.
- Narrow your focus. Begin to zero in on your mission in life.

Phase Four: Momentum & Reproduction

In this phase, God expects spiritual fruit to be produced from our lives. Phase Four usually begins in mid-life where we are no longer a mere student in God's economy. He now sees us as a "laborer" who ought to be bearing fruit for the Kingdom. This phase is a combination of phases two ("being") and three ("doing") merging together in our lives. This phase typically begins the most fruitful years of life.

Just as Joseph endured a long season of testing and Moses endured a long season of obscurity, we, too, must ready ourselves for this phase where our most productive years will occur. Often in this stage we begin to focus on our ultimate contribution in life. We know our strengths and weaknesses. We know our gifts. We know our mission. Phase Four is about a lifestyle of surrender. All things are done to advance the kingdom not ourselves.

God's Objectives for Phase Four...

◉ **Clear Priorities** – God desires that we have a definite grasp on priorities. We must be able to discern what is best and when to say "no" to things. We must be strategic planners. We are no longer slaves to the "immediate" but are giving ourselves to the "ultimate." Read Acts 6:1-4.

◉ **Fruitfulness** – God desires that we become mature in our fruitfulness. This makes us effective in our areas of service. We know how to make it happen and how to get the job done. We are productive and fruitful. Read John 15:16.

◉ **Pure Motives** – God desires that we please Him more than we please people. Our motives for ministry are key! We must do the right things for the right reasons. Our concern is to please God more than anything else. Read Matthew 6:1-6.

◉ **Spiritual Reproduction** – God desires that we be able to pass on transferable concepts to others under us. We are able to mentor and disciple others effectively and completely (Col. 1:28-29). We begin to master the issue of spiritual reproduction - we start producing disciples who produce disciples. Read 2 Timothy 2:2.

◉ **Communion as a Lifestyle** – God desires that we commune with Him on a regular basis, regardless of the hardships we face. We must be positive and teachable in our response to His life lessons. Read 2 Timothy 1:12.

◉ **Perspective in Crisis** – We are to maintain objectivity and poise by seeing life through God's eyes. Believing in a sovereign God, we can trust that He has all things under His control and that all things will ultimately be used for the good of His Kingdom and for His glory. Read Romans 8:28.

Phase Four is about a lifestyle of surrender. All things are done to advance the Kingdom, not ourselves.

Real Life...

At the turn of the 20th century, two young boys grew up together in the same neighborhood. As adults, both contracted polio, a deadly disease at the time. As they struggled with their condition, their attitudes began to polarize. One decided to give up on anything close to a normal life. He became a recluse and took a pessimistic perspective on life. Although he was the more gifted of the two, he eventually became bitter and fatalistic. The other resolved to make the most of his disease and see it as a way to identify with others enduring hardship. He made it all the way to the top. He became President Franklin D. Roosevelt.

The Construction of a Life...

As we continue our house analogy, Phase Four represents the work on the exterior of the house. The outward walls have all been put up, and everyone can see what the house has become - what it looks like. When built well, the house is not only beautiful to look at, but also provides secure covering from the weather. The structure is fully functional for others to dwell in.

Reflect and Respond...

What do you think will be most difficult for you at Phase Four? Write it down in this space so you will remember it.

Reflect
and
Respond

Describe in 15-20 words what you hope your life will look like at this phase.

Group Up

Share what challenges you see for yourself and what you hope your life will look like at this phase.

YOUR PART...

- Begin to handle isolation, conflict, and crisis with trust.
- Define your gift-mix. Your role is clear in the Body of Christ.
- Develop effective communication skills.
- Delegate to others and control your ego!
- Think through and implement a Biblical strategy for ministry.
- Understand and apply the 80/20 principle: when your priorities are right, 20% of your time is yielding 80% of your results (with wrong priorities, it is possible that 80% of your time will yield 20% of your results).

Phase Five: Convergence & Significance

The next stage is one of great fulfillment that few leaders attain. It occurs when three factors converge together:

- the leader
- the task
- the context

In other words, who we are, the work we do, and the people we do it with come together and match perfectly. Our lives flourish because all these factors have come together. Consider Bill McCartney, who left his coaching career at the University of Colorado to give leadership full time to Promise Keepers. Consider John Maxwell, who left Skyline Wesleyan Church in San Diego, California in order to devote his time to training pastors to become more effective leaders. A match occurred as these men made those moves.

God's Objectives for Phase Five...

Effectiveness – God desires us to have a leadership/ministry match that provides maximum, visible effectiveness. God will continue to test us because He is looking for deep effectiveness in our lives. His tests help us to zero in on the central legacy we are to leave.

Wisdom & Objectivity – God desires us to apply relevant knowledge to life. The more people we have influence over, the more cautiously we must make decisions in ministry. Our life experience has taught us which battles are worth fighting and which are not.

World Vision – God desires us to own a sense of destiny and embrace it. He wants us to see the whole picture of how our life and our work fit in with His overall purposes for the world.

Equipping Ability – God desires us to reproduce laborers and ministers, just as we have become ourselves. He wants us to train others with the skills and knowledge that we possess. We are more concerned now with multiplying workers than merely adding numbers to the Kingdom.

Deep Gratitude for Calling – Your motivation for work is gratitude for the place God has ultimately given you. You feel a sense that this is what you were made to do and are deeply appreciative to the God who has called and equipped you to do this work for His Kingdom.

Identity as a Coach – You draw fulfillment from coaching a team more than from playing the game yourself. You step back from the thick of the activity and coach others, empowering them to try out their skills and gifts. You direct them and cheer them on.

Group Up

Discuss what internal moves need to occur (as referred to in "A Word of Caution") for a person to progress through this stage and achieve these objectives.

A Word of Caution...

It is easy to misunderstand this phase we all long to achieve. Often a pastor will jump from church to church, trying to find the perfect ministry match. Some will even move every two to three years. Unfortunately, this is not how most will arrive at Phase Five. Frequently, it is an internal move and not an external one which God requires.

The Construction of a Life...

Phase Five represents those components in a house that are personal finishing touches, and make the house unique. They give it personality and flair. It might be adding a deck or some trim around the siding, or a patio or porch. Now the house is complete. It is grand and enables the homeowner to enjoy all the years of labor that have been put into it.

Reflect and Respond...

Think of people you know who are in this phase of life. Describe the traits that they exhibit from the list of God's objectives.

Name	Trait(s)
1.	
2.	
3.	
4.	
5.	
6.	

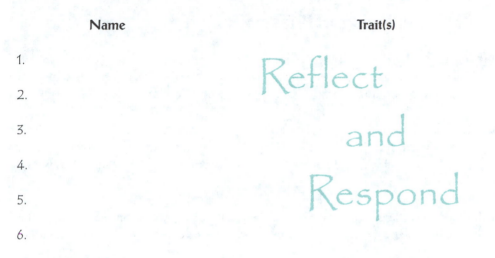

Group Up

Who did you come up with as someone who is in this phase of life?

Share and discuss with the group.

What do you admire most about them? How would you describe their lives? What person might be able to mentor you in your current phase of life? If they can mentor you, put a check in the box.

Name	Description	Mentor
1.		❑
2.		❑
3.		❑
4.		❑
5.		❑
6.		❑

YOUR PART...

- ⬥ Trust and rest in God's movement of your position (location and proximity).
- ⬥ See God's hand in the midst of trials.
- ⬥ Disciple and mentor others.
- ⬥ Surround yourself with like visionaries.
- ⬥ Work smarter rather than harder.
- ⬥ Humbly recognize that it is God who has brought you this far.

Phase Six: Afterglow & Anointing

This final phase is the ultimate goal for each one of us. It generally occurs in the twilight years of life when we are living from the overflow of our wisdom, experience, and labor. In these final years, others simply want to be around you because of the life you have lived. You carry great respect, admiration, and influence. Think about older saints you know that have entered this phase. Do you know any? It seems to me that in the 1990s, Dr. Billy Graham entered this phase. He had lived his life so well, that all who knew him held him in high esteem and honor. While Phase Six is not necessarily synonymous with fame, it certainly means that you have great influence with those who know you.

God's Objectives for Phase Six...

- **Influence** – God desires us to hold a deep and wide span of influence. At this point, we naturally mentor. We may, perhaps, even mentor from far away (others may hear about our lives, hear a tape of us speaking, or read what we have written).

- **Leadership Production** – God desires us to reproduce leaders who can lead as effectively as we have. This is the highest level of disciple-making and spiritual reproduction. Only a leader can reproduce another leader. This mentoring of other leaders becomes a fulfilling part of Phase Six.

- **Fulfillment** – God desires that we realize the reward of life is the journey itself. At this point we find deep satisfaction in just being who we are and doing what we are doing.

- **Anointing on Life** – We find ourselves walking in a life-style of blessing and anointing. The overflow of our lives impacts others, and we influence people without even trying.

- **Deadness to Flattery or Insults** – You are not easily moved by people's flattery or criticism of who you are. You have become secure in your identity, gifts, and work, and recognize that all of these are ultimately from God anyway.

- **Mentoring & Apprenticing** – You enjoy investing your life in others and spend most of your energy and effort doing so. Your concern is for the legacy you will leave behind you.

Group Up

As a group think of someone who has reached this phase.

What about their life and ministry leads you to place them in this phase?

The Construction of a Life...

By this final stage, you have grown well through the other stages. You now enjoy the results of years of quality "home improvements."

YOUR PART...

- Select and mentor sharp, potential giants.
- Reflect His glory in everything.
- Communicate from the overflow – let your heart spill over.

Reflect and Respond...

This final phase is all about finishing well. It's about a life lived well. Now give yourself the freedom to dream big. What is the vision for life that God has given you? Even if this vision is not absolutely clear to you, envision what your life might be like during this phase. Describe it.

Reflect
and
Respond

Have you caught a glimpse of the big picture? This can be an overwhelming amount of information, but knowing the full panorama encourages us within each stage. Look ahead to the end phases anytime you become discouraged with the stage you are in right now. Be encouraged to persevere. God desires the best for all His children!!!

Phase Jumping

It can be difficult to determine when we are moving from one stage to the next. Below are some hints that may give us a clue that a transition is occurring:

Common boundaries that mark beginnings of new phases . . .

- Crisis/tests

- Promotions

- Learning a major, new concept

- A new ministry

- Unusual experience

- A life-changing encounter with someone

- A geographic move

- Experiencing divine guidance

As you begin moving into new phases, you will notice . . .

- You begin holding a different sphere of influence.

- You recognize the greater importance of people.

- You experience deeper tests of obedience and leadership.

- You become relevant to new audiences.

- Others sense and recognize your growth.

"There has never been the slightest doubt in my mind that the God who started this great work in you would keep at it and bring it to a flourishing finish on the very day Christ Jesus appears."
Philippians 1:6
(The Message)

Assess Yourself...

Reflect on the six stages of growth described in this lesson. What stages have you gone through? List them in the margin or space below. Write about the experiences that brought you through each stage. What stage do you think you are in right now? Why do you think this? Write about what you are experiencing now. Be sure to include the successes and struggles of each phase. Both are part of the growth process. You may want to do this in a notebook, or another sheet of paper, or put it on your computer in your personal file.

Make the following questions a part of the above assessment.

What phases are you expecting now? Jot it down.

Evaluate what it will take for you to get to the next phase. What are the issues God wants you to address?

What truths does God want to teach you?

Based on the information that you provided above, list three specific steps that you need to take to continue your growth process - either to work through a current phase or to head toward the next phase.

1.

2.

3.

Application

Now that we have looked at each of the six phases, let's map out our personal growth. Create a time line of your life on a separate sheet of paper or on the computer. Put it where you can reference it regularly. Take some time and plot out the stages (or phases) you've walked through. Be as specific as possible. Pinpoint significant times in your life that have led to spiritual growth. Indicate the time the growth occurred and describe the events, issues, or people that sparked this growth in your life. Mark which phases you have been through, when you passed from one to another, and where you are now in your life. This exercise should take some time. It will be a great way to step back and really see the big picture of where you have been and what God has done.

The Five Levels of Leadership

WHY PEOPLE FOLLOW THEIR LEADERS

"And David shepherded them with integrity of heart, with skillful hands he led them."
Psalm 78:72

The Teacher Who Had Influence

In 1996 I remember seeing the movie *Mr. Holland's Opus*. It was a powerful movie that illustrated the influence of a man who became a leader at John F. Kennedy high school.

Mr. Holland was a musician who had no desire to make a difference in anyone's life. His goal was to go to New York and compose a symphony. He wanted to be rich and famous. He decided to become a music teacher for three years, just to save up some money to get to New York. Along the way, however, the three years turned into thirty years. He never left the school.

Just a year after taking the position, he began to build relationships with students. Some of them had great needs in their life. Reluctantly, he began to meet with them before and after school to work on their music skills. A red-haired girl met with him early to learn to play the clarinet. Soon, Mr. Holland discovered that her real need was not about clarinets, but about self-esteem. He began to encourage her and affirm her strengths. Soon, there were other students who met with him and grew under his mentoring.

Mr. Holland began to introduce musicals and productions to the school, which gave a tremendous outlet for students to develop themselves and raise money for the school. His popularity grew over the next several years.

Finally, near the end of the movie, Mr. Holland was called into the principle's office. It was one of those nightmare meetings. Due to budget cutbacks in the district, all the music classes were being cut. Mr. Holland was being fired. He was angry. He was scared. He became disillusioned. He thought to himself, "I could have gone to New York and at least had some money at this point in my life!" He felt his life had been wasted.

In the final scene of the movie, Mr. Holland was walking out of the school for the last time and heard a noise coming from the auditorium. When he opened the doors, he couldn't believe what he saw. Thirty years of students were crowded in the room – clapping as he stood at the entrance. They had returned to say thanks for making such a difference in their lives.

The governor of the state stood up at the podium. She happened to be the red-haired girl Mr. Holland had mentored thirty years earlier. She spoke: "Mr. Holland, I've heard rumors that you feel your life has been a failure because you never made it to New York and became rich or famous composing a symphony.

"You never got to New York, and never got rich or famous around here. But, Mr. Holland, if you feel you are a failure – that is where you are wrong. Just look around you." She

Basic Truth
The longer you
are a leader,
the more reasons
you should give
people to follow you.

Guided Prayer
Father, teach me
the skills and cultivate
in me a heart that
will make me into
a good shepherd and
leader for Your people.

Help me to understand
what it takes to lead
others well.

Amen.

paused. "We are your symphony!" Mr. Holland's eyes welled up with tears as he recognized he had done far more by investing in students than by scratching notes on paper. He had changed people forever.[1]

One Step at a Time

I love this movie. In it, we see an illustration of the five levels of leadership. Mr. Holland's journey with students began when he took a position. His influence was only as big as his position as a teacher. Soon, however he developed relationships, and his influence grew beyond his position. Next, he produced results for the school and won the respect of both staff and students. His influence grew even more. Soon, he found himself investing in students - and gaining even more influence. By the end of the movie, his was the story of a man whose impact was far-reaching, even though he never tried to accomplish that goal. He had successfully negotiated the five levels of leadership.

Years ago, Dr. John Maxwell created a diagram called *The Five Levels of Leadership*. It is insightful and helps us understand why people follow leaders. Just like climbing a staircase, we usually climb these steps one at a time when we begin to influence others. Let me try to explain it briefly.

The Five Levels of Leadership

5. Personhood

Respect
People follow because
of who you are and
what you represent.

4. People Development

Reproduction
People follow because of what
you have done for them.

3. Production

Results
People follow because of what
you have done for the organization.

2. Permission

Relationships
People follow because they want to.

1. Position

Rights
People follow you because they have to.

1. POSITION

The lowest level of leadership for any person is based on a title or job description. If as a student you follow a leader only because he is named professor or she is the team leader, then that person is a positional leader. People follow only because they have to. Your influence on this level will not extend beyond the lines of your job description. The only authority you have is what your title gives you.

Position

| Respect |
| Reproduction |
| Results |
| Relationships |
| Rights |

Most of the time, leadership begins at the positional level. But leadership that stays on this level for long becomes weaker, not stronger. Leaders who want others to follow simply because they are "the professor" soon lose the respect of their people. The longer you stay at this level, the higher the turnover and the lower the morale of the people.

Growing Beyond a Position

The story of Prince Charles and Princess Diana is a tragic one. They married in 1981. It was called the Wedding of the Century. Within a decade, they were separated. Soon, they divorced. Diana lost her title as Princess of Wales. Her influence, however, was not lost. In fact, her influence continued to grow long after she lost the throne. She became a spokesperson for children, along with speaking out against AIDS, and the use of land mines. Although it was her position that gave her a place of influence, she didn't require a position to grow in her influence.

Interestingly, Prince Charles' story is very different. If he lost his position, the world would not remember him as they have Diana. He has not won the hearts of people or built relationships like Diana did. If he lost his royal position, he would likely lose his influence as well.

In my opinion, one person grew beyond her position, the other did not. Prince Charles is dependent on his position to have influence, Diana was not. Diana moved to the next level; Charles never moved from this level of positional leadership.

You may know someone like Charles. They have a position, but they have no influence outside of it. They may be in student government, a campus ministry leader, or a Resident Assistant. Yet when you see them interact with others, no one follows them beyond their job description requirements. They're totally relying on a position to have any clout.

One thing is sure. Your boss can give you authority, but he cannot give you influence. People follow best when you earn a place of influence.

Reflect and Respond...

Do you know a leader who is leading merely on the grounds of their title? In your opinion, how effective are they as a leader?

Reflect and Respond

Respect

Reproduction

Results

Relationships

Rights

Group Up

Discuss the ways that you gain permission from people to lead.

How do you do this practically?

2. PERMISSION

The next level of leadership is based on the relationships of a leader with the people. As followers grow to like and trust a leader, they begin to follow beyond the leader's stated authority. They follow because they want to.

When you have people's permission to lead, the whole leadership process becomes more enjoyable for everyone. Yet positive relationships alone aren't strong enough to create lasting leadership. There is a sense of family that arises in the organization. The care and the conversation do not merely revolve around the work to be done. The leader demonstrates a concern for the personal lives of the followers.

He Knows Me!

Napoleon Bonaparte, was a military leader who eventually became Emperor of France. During his early years, he attempted to know all of his soldiers by name. You can imagine the impact this had on them. By the time he became emperor, his army had grown much too large to remember all their names, so he simply got familiar with every officer in his army. He liked to wander through the camp, meet an officer, greet him by name and talk about his hometown, wife and family. However, he never wanted to lose touch with the common soldier who fought for him. So, he came up with a plan to create this sense of family and make each man feel special.

After each battle, he would approach the officer in charge and ask him for the name of a soldier who had fought hard in the battle, but had not received much credit. When the officer gave him the name of someone, Napoleon would inquire about this man's wife, hometown and family. Then, as he inspected the troops the next day, and at the signal of his officer, Napoleon would single out this soldier and congratulate him on the great job he did in the battle. Then, he would ask about his wife and kids and chat for a moment. Afterward, the rest of the army would gather around this man, amazed that the Emperor had such relationship and knowledge of his troops. It is no wonder Napoleon garnered such loyalty from his men. Everyone felt honored to be there!

Even a tyrant like Napoleon understood the necessity of relationships in leadership. He worked at building as many positive relationships as he could, even when he became Emperor. He drew fierce loyalty from others because of the relationships he built and the trust he earned.

Reflect and Respond...

How are your relational skills? Is this a level you anticipate you may struggle with?

I Need You, Jim

John Maxwell tells the story of his days as a pastor in Ohio. A 65 year-old man named Jim was the most influential man in the church. Unfortunately, he was extremely negative. He had run the last two pastors off and his attitude affected the atmosphere of the whole church.

So when Pastor Maxwell arrived, he arranged a meeting with Jim. In that meeting, John said to him: "Jim, I have heard that you have a lot of influence in this church. I've also heard that you have been very negative about the last two pastors. That's why I wanted to meet with you right away to make an offer to you."

"For the next few years, you will have more influence than me in this church. During that time, you can make things horrible for me as a young pastor. We can fight and argue until I eventually win enough new people to Christ and invite enough new people to this church that I begin to have as much influence as you. Then, I'll begin to win some of those fights. The future of this church will sway back and forth at that point. We will make each other miserable."

"Jim, it looks to me like you have a choice in front of you. You can literally spend the last years of your life fighting with me or you can accept my invitation to you. My offer is, let's work together. I will meet with you every Tuesday and discuss the issues of the church. I will get your counsel on everything. Together, we can make these next years the most fruitful years in our church's history. I need you, Jim. The choice is yours."

Jim simply got up and walked out the door. Pastor Maxwell followed him, not knowing if he was leaving for good. Jim stopped at the drinking fountain and got a drink, for what seemed like an eternity. When he stood up, his face was red. Tears were streaming down his cheeks. He looked at John Maxwell, and gave him a huge bear hug. Then, he said, "You can count on me, Pastor. I'm in your corner."[2]

Jim was a changed man after that. People in the church wondered what happened to him. I'll tell you what happened. Jim met a leader who had the character, security and humility to confront him in a redemptive way.

Unfortunately, many leaders stop at this level. They feel if they just become a good buddy to their people, all will be well. Wrong. Friendships don't necessarily accomplish the mission, solve the problems, or pay the expenses. Nor do they always challenge others to reach their potential.

If you stay too long on this level without rising, you will cause highly motivated people to become restless. To begin reaping the rewards of positive leadership, you have to go to the next level.

Reflect and Respond...

Have you witnessed a leader who tried to maintain their influence merely by their relationships with others? What happened? Were they a successful leader? Share your thoughts with others if you are comfortable doing so.

Reflect
and
Respond

3. PRODUCTION

At the production level, influence is cemented and respect is increased because of what the leader and the people accomplish together. This is where success is sensed by most people. They like you and what you are doing. Problems are fixed with little effort because of momentum. People begin to follow because of what the leader has done for the team or organization. If you reach this level, you and your team can achieve many of your goals. But to experience life-changing impact and lasting success, you have to make the leap to the next level.

A Tale of Two Women

The story of the Underground Railroad is incredible. It was a secret route from the South to the North during the days of the Civil War in America where more than 300 slaves were ushered into freedom.

The leader of this Underground Railroad was a tiny woman named Harriet Tubman. If you had seen her, your first reaction might not have been one of respect. She wasn't impressive looking - just a little over five feet tall with weathered skin. She couldn't read or write. She was a minority. Her smile revealed two front teeth were missing. She had no title except those she earned as nicknames leading slaves in the night. She had no funding. She had no authority given to her by anyone when she started. She simply got the job done. She led hundreds of slaves into freedom, who might not have ever made it on their own.

She was so effective that people of prominence sought her out including William Seward, Frederick Douglas, and John Brown. Brown called her "General Tubman," and said later that she "was a better officer than most whom he had seen and could command an army as successfully as she had led her small parties of fugitives."[3]

Another tiny woman worth noting was Mother Teresa, missionary to Calcutta. She started as a Catholic teacher in a girls' school in Calcutta. While teaching, she kept looking out the window at the impoverished people on the streets. She knew she had to do something about them.

She approached her priest and asked if she could be sent out to serve the poor. Her request was denied. She persisted saying she saw Jesus on the faces of the poor and dying. The administration finally allowed her to go. She was released with no funding.

She began to pick up bodies of dying people and care for them. Soon, she got a building and was even able to care for a Hindu leader in the community. Her influence grew. By 1979, she had won a Nobel Peace Prize for her work. She remained in Calcutta until she died in 1997, where her work lives on. She led the largest order of its kind anywhere in the world.

These two women led others effectively despite their lack of resources, despite their minority status, and despite their lack of a title. Why? They got the job done. Everyone saw them as competent leaders, driven by a cause.

Reflect and Respond...

Have you been a part of an organization where you experienced the success and results of a leader who was on the production level? What did it feel like? Write down what it feels like to you.

4. PEOPLE DEVELOPMENT

The highest calling of any leader is to help other leaders reach their potential. Leaders who move up to the people development level change their focus. They go from inspiring and leading followers to developing and leading other leaders. As a result, people respect you not only for what you've done for the team, but also for what you've done for them personally. You don't simply minister to others, you mentor them. This is where long range growth occurs. Your commitment to developing leaders will insure ongoing growth to the team and to individuals. You are no longer satisfied with simply adding to the organization's growth, but rather multiplying it!

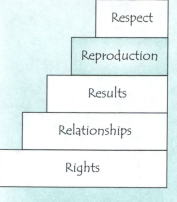

| Respect |
| Reproduction |
| Results |
| Relationships |
| Rights |

I Wanna be Like You...

Dawson Trotman is a beautiful example of this fourth level of people development and the multiplication factor. "Daws" was the founder of The Navigators, a worldwide ministry committed to making disciples. Early in his ministry, a young sailor approached Daws and asked for help with personal growth. Daws clarified that what the sailor was really asking for was to be discipled. He then agreed to do it over the next several months. During the experience, this sailor's life was so dramatically changed that he brought a buddy of his to Daws and asked if Daws would disciple him as well. The reply startled both of the sailors: "Absolutely not." Then, Daws went on to say, "If your friend is going to be discipled, it will have to be you who does it." So the two of them connected in a discipleship relationship. Upon their completion, the chain continued. Both went out and found someone in whom they could invest their lives. This happened again and again and again and again.[4]

What makes this story so intriguing is that it literally transformed the atmosphere on the ship. Eventually, the F.B.I. was called in to investigate what was going on. Some thought a cult had broken out. Others wondered about the odd behavior of what was once a normal group of sailors. Clearly, things were different. What's more, once the F.B.I. began to investigate, it took them six months to sift through all the men who had been discipled in order to find Daws – the one who had started the whole thing. That is one thick web of disciples! What an encouraging snapshot of what can happen if we become serious about multiplying.

Reflect and Respond...

After understanding the difference between the results level and reproduction level, why do you think it is important for a leader to go beyond the results level to this next level? Share your thoughts here.

1.

2.

3.

Group Up

Discuss this idea of people development.

How exactly do you raise up other leaders?

Come up with ways that one goes about developing people.

5. PERSONHOOD

The fifth and highest level of leadership is personhood. It is the true respect level. Leaders who spend their lives developing people and organizations make such an incredible impact for so long that people follow because of who the leader is and what he represents. Few make it to this level. It is the result of being faithful and fruitful for a long time, in an arena that counts. The leader seeks significance, not success. At this level, the leader has produced results and everyone can see his or her impact. To get to this level, you must work faithfully through the first four levels with as many as you can with the purpose of adding value to their lives. If you do that your whole life, the rest will take care of itself.

Personhood

Jesus' IDEA

How do we reach the Personhood level of leadership? Good question. First, we need to recognize it takes many years. You may reach this level in your campus leadership, but you will embark on a whole new world once you graduate. Give yourself time to mature. Second, we need to recognize that our goal should simply be to imitate our Lord. How did Jesus reach this level with His staff? Let's take a look.

Have you ever read the Gospels, and seen Jesus as a mentor, as well as a Savior? He consistently developed others, particularly His twelve disciples. If you look closely, you can see there were four training tools He used over and over. This is Jesus' IDEA of how to develop people into leaders:

I - Instruction... in a life-related context.
Jesus verbally taught His disciples all the principles they needed to know. Can you think of some examples of how He did this? Jot one or two in the margin.

D - Demonstration... in a life-related context.
Jesus didn't stop with instruction. He modeled the life He wanted them to emulate. He set the leadership example. Can you think of examples of how He did this?

E - Experience... in a life-related context.
Jesus then gave His twelve real experience. The disciples got to do it themselves. Participation leads to application. Can you think of examples of how He did this?

A - Assessment... in a life-related context.
Finally, Jesus provided feedback and accountability. He assessed how well His disciples were doing as they learned. Can you think of examples of how He did this?

Reflect and Respond...

What leaders can you point to that have reached Personhood? Why do you attribute this level to their leadership? Write down the name(s) of those who have reached this level for you.

Reflect and Respond

Group Up

Share which leaders you came up with who are at this level.

Deborah's Climb Up

Deborah is a classic example of a person who climbed up the the Five Levels of Leadership. She is remarkable especially because so few women were given leadership positions during her day. Men did not naturally follow women. However, she commanded the respect of both men and women because of her leadership gifts. Even Barak, the military commander of the northern tribes of Israel sought her help when she challenged him to attack Canaan. In fact, he accepted the challenge on the condition that she would join him. Even though Barak's need for a woman would eclipse any honor due him if he defeated Canaan, he still wanted her next to him. Together they defeated the enemy. She combined both care and courage which won her the respect of everyone. Clearly, Deborah illustrated the qualities of one who has climbed the steps of leadership: she was the strongest leader of her day. Even the other recognized leaders in Israel followed her.

Reflect and Respond...

Read Judges 4–5. What qualities do you see in Deborah that made her a good leader?

1.

2.

3.

4.

5.

Reflect
and
Respond

Group Up
Discuss the leadership qualities you discovered in your study of Deborah.

Steps Deborah Took

In reading Judges 4–5, we can see very clearly Deborah's progress from one level to the next up the Five Levels of Leadership. Follow along as we walk through this progression. In observing Deborah, we notice the following:

☙ She secured a position.
"Deborah, the wife of Lappidoth, was a prophet..." (4:4, NLT).

As we said before all leadership begins on the position level. That's where Deborah began – as a prophetess.

☙ She gained the people's permission.
"...who had become a judge in Israel. She would hold court under the Palm of Deborah, which stood between Ramah and Bethel in the hill country of Ephraim, and the Israelites came to her to settle their disputes" (4:4–5, NLT).

When Deborah gained the trust of the people as a prophet, she became a judge. And because Scripture says people came to her, we know she had their permission to influence them.

She produced results.

"She sent for Barak son of Abinoam from Kedesh in Naphtali and said to him, 'The Lord, the God of Israel, commands you: Go, take with you ten thousand men of Naphtali and Zebulun and lead the way to Mount Tabor. I will lure Sisera, the commander of Jabin's army, with his chariots and his troops, to the Kishon River and give him into your hands.'... On that day God subdued Jabin, the Canaanite king, before the Israelites. An d the hand of the Israelites grew stronger and stronger against Jabin, until they destroyed him" (Judg. 4:6-7, 23-24).

The people of Israel experienced freedom from the oppression of King Jabin as a result of Deborah's leadership. She not only explained the job ahead of them, but she provided the tools necessary to accomplish it. She didn't simply tell Barak to go and fight, but she furnished a game plan for the attack and gave him 10,000 troops from two of the tribes of Israel to do it. Barak had every resource he needed to win, and what a win it was for the people of Israel! Her influence was cemented and respect for her increased because of the success they experienced together.

She began developing people.

"So Deborah went with Barak to Kedesh, where he summoned Zebulun and Naphtali. Ten thousand men followed him, and Deborah also went with him" (Judg. 4:9-10).

Deborah understood that her success as a leader was not measured merely by the results she produced, but by the people she developed. And that's exactly what Deborah did. She helped Barak achieve his God-given purpose as a leader. Because she did this, other rulers and princes were successful (Judg. 5:14-15), thousands of men became instruments in God's hands, and hundreds of thousands of people enjoyed the fruit of her leadership.

She became a "mother" for her nation.

"Village life in Israel ceased, ceased until I, Deborah, arose, arose a mother in Israel." (Judg. 5:7).

We don't have a long record of Deborah's accomplishments, but the fact that she was recorded as a "mother of Israel" seems to indicate that she achieved personhood.

Reflect and Respond...

Why do you think that moving from one level to the next is so important as a leader? Can a leader stay at a certain level of leadership without moving all the way up and still be successful?

Reflect

and

Respond

Climbing the Steps of Leadership

The following are truths that will enable you to better interpret "The Five Levels of Leadership" diagram. Consider each, as you think about what level you are on with the college students you lead.

- **The higher you go, the longer it takes.**

- **The higher you go, the higher the level of commitment.**

- **The higher you go, the easier it is to lead.**

- **The higher you go, the greater the growth.**

- **You never leave the base level, or the levels below where you are.**

- **As a leader, you won't be on the same level with all of your people.**

- **You must work to carry other leaders with you up the steps.**

Group Up

Take some time to discuss the statements to the left under "Climbing the Steps of Leadership."

Why are they true?

What is the significance of each statement?

HOW DO WE CLIMB THE LEADERSHIP STEPS?

Here are some ways that you can begin your assent in the levels of leadership:

- ◇ Consistently ask God to build you into a more effective leader.

- ◇ Develop confidence in your people skills.

- ◇ See every relationship you have as a chance to develop that person.

- ◇ Walk slowly through the crowds.

- ◇ Constantly keep a list of potential leaders you can invest in.

- ◇ Prioritize discipleship: find systematic ways to train people.

- ◇ Select and develop (mentor) key leaders.

- ◇ Live a model life that others would want to imitate.

- ◇ Recognize that people are your most valuable asset.

Guided Prayer

Dear God,
help me begin this
climb up the steps
to greater leadership
development.

Give me perspective
to remember that
becoming a leader is
a daily process, not
something that will be
accomplished in a day.

May I invest in the
things that matter to
You, Your people and
Your Kingdom work.

Amen.

It Works for Me!

I joined the staff at Skyline Church in San Diego in 1983. Dr. John Maxwell was the senior pastor. I was the Collegiate Pastor, with a department of about 60 students. I am thankful that John Maxwell saw potential in me, because he took me under his wing and began to develop me as a leader. He taught me leadership and the genius of developing the people around me. It was a win/win situation. Within seven years, our department grew from an average of 60 students to 600 students. Further, there are now 402 graduates in full-time ministry around the world, who were developed as leaders in that department. What John Maxwell started in me has impacted every one of those students indirectly as they serve globally. That's the power of multiplication!

I have a question for you. Are you multiplying yet? Where are you in the Five Levels of Leadership? When you look at the big picture, do you see yourself making progress in your leadership? My hope is that you will climb these steps and impact your world.

Assess Yourself

How influential are you as a leader? Why do you think this is? rate yourself on a scale from 1 to 10 with "1" being the lowest and "10" being the highest. Put a mark on the line.

```
+----+----+----+----+----+----+----+----+----+
1    2    3    4    5    6    7    8    9    10
```

Which of the five levels are you at currently in your leadership? What indications lead you to place yourself there? What steps will you take to push yourself to the next level?

Are you living out the highest calling of a leader by training other leaders? If not, who can you begin investing in and developing right now? List ways you will do this.

Application

List all the people you presently lead. Then, after their name, write down what level of leadership you are on, in your relationship with them. In other words, why is it they follow you? Is it only because you have some position? Is it because you have a good relationship with them? Is it because of the results you've produced? Is it because you have equipped (mentored) them as a leader?

Then, write out what step you need to take with each person, in order to climb to the next level of leadership with them.

When will you take this step? Who will hold you accountable?

Stay in Character

THE FIRST INGREDIENT OF LEADERSHIP

"Do you not know that in a race all the runners run, but only one gets the prize? Run in such a way as to get the prize. Everyone who competes in the games goes into strict training. They do it to get a crown that will not last; but we do it to get a crown that will last forever. Therefore I do not run like a man running aimlessly; I do not fight like a man beating the air. No, I beat my body and make it my slave so that after I have preached to others, I myself will not be disqualified for the prize."
I Corinthians 9:24-27

Stay in Character!

Every year at our church in San Diego, we performed the "Living Christmas Tree." It was a huge production, and some years we made it fun by bringing in live animals for the nativity seen. Unfortunately, the live animals did not always behave as we would want them to during a performance. As you would probably guess, the animals had a few "accidents" at very inappropriate times! As the choir on stage was laughing at the scenes before them, the director would scold, "Stay in character!" No matter how crazy things became on stage, it was imperative that the singers stayed in character.

And so it is with us. Life will throw us curve balls that we did not plan for. Yet, good or bad, God calls us to continue living as we know we should live. Our job is to follow the script (Scripture) and to stay in character! Character is the first ingredient of leadership.

How Important Is It?

In the 1990s, the subject of character became a front burner item in the minds of almost everyone. The big debate during the Clinton scandals asked, Does character count? Can someone be a good leader without it? The answer, of course is yes...for a short while. Leaders soon learn that strategic thinking or charisma is helpful, but if they fail to develop character, they will eventually sabotage their leadership. Ability may get you to the top, but it takes character to keep you there!

In a 1996 survey, students considered moral decline the biggest problem facing America, as well as the number one issue facing teenagers. Ironically, 76% of them admitted they were guilty of cheating. The majority of them have no qualms about lying. Hmmm.... Where do they get this attitude? Are you in the majority?

The First Ingredient of Leadership

Basic Truth
Character is the framework that enables us to do what is right even when it is difficult.

Guided Prayer
Father, I know that what matters most is what is on the inside of me – who I am as a person.

Yet, too often I am more concerned with what is on the outside – my image and how people see me.

Help me to develop and grow on the inside as a person of character and integrity, so that I naturally reflect integrity in what I say and do.

Amen.

What We Learned from the Top

In August 1998, we learned from our President that expediency rules. Say whatever you need to say to stay in office. Lie if you have to because later you can redefine what your words meant. Truth is relative. When you're finally forced to confess to immorality, you don't actually have to apologize. Just tell people it is time to move on. After all, the economy is good.

In the speech President Clinton gave, where he admitted to lying about his affair with a White House intern, he invested an interesting amount of time on the issues. The speech totaled 549 words. Note the number of words devoted to the following:

- Words devoted to self-justification: 134
- Words devoted to regret for his actions: 4
- Words devoted to attack on the prosecutor: 180
- Words devoted to saying it's time to move on: 137
- Words devoted to apology: 0

Group Up

Discuss what it means to be a person of character.

After that speech, most Americans agreed that something was conspicuously absent. We all know good leadership when we see it, and when we don't. Things might have been different had President Clinton said: "I take full responsibility for my actions. I blame no one. I acted immorally and I lied about it to my country. I have wronged my wife. I have wronged my daughter. I have wronged America. As your leader, I apologize and seek your forgiveness." As a leader, President Clinton was loaded with charisma. What America needed from their leader in that moment, however, wasn't charisma - we needed character.

History teaches us that America is very forgiving to a leader who owns up to his or her actions. Just ask John F. Kennedy. After his biggest presidential mistake, The Bay of Pigs fiasco, he assumed full responsibility for it. His popularity actually went up. In fact, he said, "I don't understand it. The more mistakes I make, the more they like me!"

It wasn't his mistakes that drew Americans to him. It was the exhibition of integrity. People felt they could trust him. Someone was taking responsibility.

Reflect and Respond...

What do you understand good character to be? Do you think you cannot sustain your leadership without it?

Reflect

and

Respond

The Book of Virtues

Many school districts nationwide have introduced character training into their curriculum. Most adults have finally agreed that good character is a prerequisite to good conduct. William Bennett felt compelled to write his book, *The Book of Virtues*, in the midst of our character crisis.

In his book he suggests we develop ten virtues:

1. Self-discipline	6. Courage
2. Compassion	7. Perseverance
3. Responsibility	8. Honesty
4. Friendship	9. Loyalty
5. Strong work ethic	10. Faith

Big on the Inside

At a county fair a few years ago, a man encountered a little girl with a huge mass of cotton candy on a paper cone. He asked, "How can a little girl like you eat all of that cotton candy?"

"Well, you see, Mister," she answered. "I'm really much bigger on the inside than I am on the outside!"

That's exactly the kind of leaders God wants to raise up! Those whose substance is bigger than their image. Good character is to be praised more than outstanding talent. Most talents, are, to some extent, a gift. Good character, by contrast, is not given to us. We must build it piece by piece – through thought, choice, courage, and determination.

Character Defined

Let me suggest a definition of character for us as disciples of Jesus.

Simply put, I believe that character is

The sum total of our identity, emotional security, core values, and self-discipline.

First, we must settle the issue of our IDENTITY. A strong moral compass comes only from a person who has settled who they are in Christ. When they are secure in this identity as a "new creature in Christ" they don't have to play games or get defensive about their reputation. They don't have to prove anything. They don't have to hide anything. This breeds trust among others.

Second, we must settle the issue of our EMOTIONAL SECURITY. We discussed this in session 3 entitled, "Becoming a Person of Influence." When leaders have emotional deficits, they sabotage their own leadership. Others withdraw. They sense the leader is unstable. And they are right. Insecurity is the cause of more leadership breakdowns than anything else. Emotional stability is like the infrastructure that holds a leader up in crisis.

Third, we must settle the issue of our CORE VALUES. Leaders must be principle centered. They can't drift with the culture, and change the foundation on which they stand morally or spiritually. Our core values are the horsepower that drive each decision we make. They

Character is the sum total of our identity, emotional security, core values, and self-discipline.

define who we are as a leader. They are like the rudder on a ship that keeps it on course, even in storms. Values include the ethics and principles we stand for and stand on.

Finally, we must settle the issue of SELF-DISCIPLINE. We must determine we will lead our own lives well, before we can expect anyone else to follow. As Paul says in I Timothy 3:5, "If anyone does not know how to manage his own family, how can he take care of God's church?" If you do not have your own house in order, how can you expect to help others manage theirs? A leader with self-discipline lives out the convictions he or she espouses and gains credibility among the people who observe in the leader that word and action go hand-in-hand.

Group Up

Share with the group, as you feel comfortable, where you are at with each of the elements comprising character - identity, emotional security, core values, and self-discipline.

When Leaders Lack Character

A boy named Schiklewuber, grew up one hundred years ago in Europe. As a young man, his parents never talked to him about character. He was never taught right from wrong. He wasn't hugged or valued. One night, he heard his mom and dad argue about moving away. He was convinced they hated him and suspected they were going to leave him behind. He put an emotional wall up. From then on, he would fend for himself and look out for number one. This boy grew up to be a man. The man grew up to be a leader. You know him as Adolf Hitler.

Another young boy from a Jewish family grew up in Germany during the nineteenth century. His father was nominally committed to his faith and character, but only when it was financially profitable for him. When the family moved to a new town, it was not big enough to have its own synagogue. The father decided he would give up on his faith and join some other group where he could network with clients. The young boy never forgot his father's hypocrisy. He began to see spiritual faith as only a crutch. Money ruled the world. This young boy grew up into a philosopher whose views have been adopted by entire nations. His name was Karl Marx. His communist theories have robbed individuals of freedom for almost one hundred years.

These two boys were never instilled with character and became men whose leadership was responsible for some of the most horrible atrocities and oppression in the 20th century. Character is not a small matter for any person, but it is critical for a leader. Without it, a leader is headed for disaster, and unfortunately they may take others with them.

We Cannot Rise Above the Limits of Our Character

Stephen Covey communicates very well the importance of character in the following passage:

"If I try to use human influence strategies and tactics of how to get other people to do what I want, to work better, to be more motivated, to like me and each other - while my character is fundamentally flawed, marked by duplicity or insincerity - then, in the long run, I cannot be successful. My duplicity will breed distrust, and everything I do - even using so-called good human relations techniques will be perceived as manipulative.

"It simply makes no difference how good the rhetoric is or even how good the intentions are; if there is little or no trust, there is no foundation for permanent success. Only basic goodness gives life to technique."[1]

Reflect and Respond...

With which issues of character do you wrestle?

Do you have a strong personal identity, or do you struggle with who you are?

How emotionally secure are you?

List some of your core values?

Reflect and Respond

Are you a disciplined person?   ❑ yes   ❑ no   ❑ most of the time (check one)
What disciplines are a part of your life and daily routine?

Survey of Christian Leaders

A survey was taken among pastors and Christian leaders in the United States who had fallen morally. Several hundred pastors were interviewed who had compromised their integrity, fallen into sin, and had lost their ministry. Three consistent observations were made when they responded to the question, "Why did you do it?" The three top responses were:

⋄ I had stopped spending time alone with God each day.

⋄ I had no accountability to others in my life.

⋄ I never thought this kind of sin and failure could happen to me.

How to Catch a Wolf

Some Eskimo communities have crude ways of killing wolves that stalk their areas. At night, they coat a double-edged knife with blood, and freeze it. Then, they add a second and third coat of blood, and freeze it. Before they go to bed, they stick the knife into the ice, with the blade pointing upward. As the wolves sniff the blood, they are attracted to it. They begin to lick it off, becoming more passionate as they get down to the second and first coat. Finally, trying to get the last ounce of blood off the knife, the wolves cut their own tongues and don't realize they're licking their own blood. Needless to say, by morning, the Eskimos awaken to find the wolves dead, from loss of blood.

This may sound horrifying to you, but it illustrates what happens to leaders who become consumed with their own sin. It seems wonderful at first, but soon they are trapped by it, and don't even realize it is killing them (Jas. 1:14–16).

Reflect and Respond...

Has there been a time when you or a leader you knew failed to exhibit character? What was the result? Write it down here if you are comfortable doing so.

Reflect

and

Respond

The Weakness of the Great Wall of China

The Great Wall of China is one of the Seven Wonders of the World. Do you know its history? It was originally built centuries ago to keep out all invading armies. It was built so tall and so wide, no army could penetrate it. At least, that's what they thought. The Chinese were successfully invaded three times in the first one hundred years. In none of the instances, however, did the enemy climb the wall or tunnel through it. In every case, they simply bribed the guards at the gate!

What an illustration for us today. We spend so much time, effort, and money attempting to create programs to solve our problems. We work on the "outside" to prevent anything bad from happening. Unfortunately, we fail to address the real need in our hearts. What would have happened if the Chinese had spent as much time building the character of the young men at the gates as they did the walls themselves?

Group Up

Discuss the reasons given under "The Credibility Test" as to why integrity is so important to leaders.

What do you understand each of these reasons to mean?

THE CREDIBILITY TEST

The more credible you are the more confidence people will place in you, and consequently, allow you to influence their lives. Credibility with people starts with integrity – people must trust you before they will act on your words.

Reasons why integrity is so important to leaders:
- Leadership functions on the basis of TRUTH.
- Integrity has high influence VALUE.
- Our tendency is to work harder on our IMAGE than on our integrity.
- Integrity means LIVING it myself, before leading others.
- A charismatic personality may draw people, but only INTEGRITY will keep them.
- Integrity is a VICTORY not a gift.
- You will only BECOME what you are becoming – right now!
- Leaders are to live by a higher STANDARD than followers.

Samson's Folly that Led to His Fall

To build trust, a leader must be a person of strong character. People will forgive occasional mistakes based on ability, especially if they can see that you're still growing as a leader. But they won't trust someone who has slips in character. In that area, even occasional lapses are lethal. No leader can break trust with his people and expect to keep influencing them. . . . Trust makes leadership possible. Samson learned the hard way that trust is the foundation for all genuine leadership. He is a good example of a bad leader. He was impetuous, volatile, lustful, emotional, and very unpredictable. His biceps were strong but his backbone was weak. He eventually got to a point in his leadership where he could not control his own power. No one could trust him so no one followed his leadership.

☺ **He Failed to Address Glaring Character Weaknesses.**
"One day Samson went to the Philistine city of Gaza and spend the night with a prostitute." (Judg. 16:1, NLT)

Samson struggled with sexual impurity. Because his desires were unrestrained, he continually went out of bounds. He disobeyed God's command by requesting a Philistine wife, he slept with prostitutes, and ultimately he was destroyed through his relationship with Delilah.

Anytime a leader neglects to repair flaws in his character, they become worse. Inevitably the flaws lead to a downward spiral culminating in the destruction of the leader's moral foundation.

☺ **He Counted on Deception to Safeguard Himself.**
"So Delilah said to Samson, 'Please tell me what makes you so strong and what it would take to tie you up securely.' Samson replied, 'If I am tied up with seven new bowstrings that have not yet been dried, I will be as weak as anyone else...'" (Judg. 16:6–10, NLT)

When people flirt with disobedience, they often find themselves using deception to protect themselves. That was certainly true of Samson. He was fond of using riddles to try to outwit others. He wasn't completely forthright, which later led to distrust and betrayal from the Jews.

☺ **He Acted Impulsively.**
"'Because you did this,' Samson vowed, 'I will take my revenge on you, and I won't stop until I am satisfied!' So he attacked the Philistines with great fury and killed many of them." (Judg. 15:7–8a, NLT)

Time after time, Samson displayed his impetuosity. He chose his wife rashly. He made wagers without thinking. And more than once he found himself in a bloody battle because of his impulsive spirit. A leader who cannot control his temper is a danger to himself and others.

☺ **He was Overcome Because of an Area of Weakness.**
"Then Delilah pouted, 'How can you say you love me when you don't confide in me? You've made fun of me three times now, and you still haven't told me what makes you so strong!' So day after day she nagged him until he couldn't stand it any longer. Finally, Samson told her his secret..." (Judg. 16:15–17, NLT)

Those who give free rein to their sins are eventually consumed by them. When Samson encountered Delilah, he finally met his match. Ironically, the master of deception, who toyed with others, was deceived himself by a woman. Women were his achilles heal. The deceiver was deceived; the seducer, seduced. He played a dangerous game, which he lost, and it cost him everything.

Some believe that private imperfections won't have public consequences, but they always do. What is done in the dark comes out in the light. Good actions build character in a leader and trust in the people. Bad ones undermine their work until there's no solid ground left to stand on.

◑ He Misused His God-Given Gifts.

"'I really thought you hated her,' her father explained, 'so I gave her in marriage to your best man...' Then (Samson) went out and caught three hundred foxes. He tied their tails together in pairs, and he fastened a torch to each pair of tails. Then he lit the torches and let the foxes run through the fields of the Philistine. He burned all their grain to the ground... 'Who did this?' the Philistines demanded. 'Samson,' was the reply, 'because his father-in-law from Timnah gave Samson's wife to be married to his best man.' So the Philistines went and got the woman and her father and burned them to death." (Judg. 15:2-6, NLT)

Samson possessed immense strength and godly anointing, but he took both for granted. Many times Samson exploited his God-given gift that was intended for the deliverance of His people, for the purpose of personal revenge.

God gives gifts for His own purposes, and the gifts are always greater than the person who possesses them. When a leader misuses the gifts God provides, there are always consequences.

Group Up

Explore ways that as a leader you can avoid the traps that Samson fell into due to his lack of character.

Reflect and Respond...

Are any of these signs of trouble seen in Samson present in your life? Think what you can do to reverse this sign.

Reflect

Do you depend more on your strong talents to get you through or on your strong character? Why? Check one.
- ❑ Strong Talents
- ❑ Strong Character

and

Respond

How can you avoid becoming a leader like Samson, who had so much potential and talent yet squandered it?

ALARM BELLS FOR LEADERS

Integrity is not so much what we do as much as who we are. Since we must check ourselves in this area of our character, let me give you a list of "alarm bells" that may signal a need for you to address the stability of your own integrity. This list was inspired by Charles Blair's excellent book *The Man Who Could Do No Wrong*.[2] First, let's note the following four observations about leaders and credibility:

- ◇ Every leader has weaknesses.

- ◇ Leaders are in front-line spiritual battle and are vulnerable to attacks.

- ◇ Leaders are to set a higher standard for themselves than their followers.

- ◇ Mistakes can be avoided if the leader will listen to the "alarm bells" in their life.

Questions that Ring as Alarm Bells for Leaders

1. Is my personal walk with God up-to-date?

I have accountability partners that I meet with on a regular basis.

I gave them permission to ask me: "What is the Lord teaching you lately? Do you have a fresh word from the Lord today?" As leaders, we often get so busy leading others we forget our own personal life. We're like the "starving baker." We are so busy baking bread for others, we forget to eat ourselves!

Reflect and Respond...

How regularly are you spending time with God in the Word and in prayer? Are you growing in your relationship with God? In what ways? Share 3-4 here.

1.

2.

3.

4.

Reflect

and

Respond

Group Up

Share the ways in which you are cultivating your relationship with God.

Encourage and hold one another accountable in this area.

2. Am I keeping my priorities straight?

This was a tough one for the priest, Eli, in 1 Samuel 3:12-14. He succeeded in his career, but failed as a father to his sons. He neglected his priorities. This is tempting for all of us. We tend to do the "urgent" things instead of the "important" things. We react to things that scream for our attention. Sadly, when we forget the ultimate, we become slaves to the immediate.

Reflect and Respond...

List your top five priorities. Are these reflected as priorities in your life and schedule? What do you need to adjust to make sure that you are keeping your priorities straight?

1.

2.

3.

4.

5.

Group Up

What has worked in helping you maintain your priorities?

Share your thoughts with the group.

3. Am I asking myself the hard questions?

As a leader, I must continue to ask the hard questions, such as: Why am I doing this? Do I have selfish motives? How am I doing this? Am I doing God's will my way? When am I doing this? Am I jumping ahead of God? Moses struggled with this early on. He killed an Egyptian man one day. His motives were wrong. His timing was wrong. He was attempting to do God's will his way.

Reflect and Respond...

What are the hard questions you need to ask yourself? Ask them now.

4. Am I accountable to someone in authority?

I already mentioned I have some accountability partners I meet with regularly. We have each shared five personal weaknesses we need the others to ask us about. This group is a safe group. We love each other and are full of both grace and truth. We confess our sins and faults freely to each other and are honest. Accountability is not complex. It is helping each other keep our commitments to God. This is the backbone of the collegiate discipleship strategy called "CrossSeekers."

Reflect and Respond...

Are you accountable to anyone? If so, write down their name and the areas where they do or could hold you accountable. If not, commit to finding someone within the next two weeks who can serve this role in your life. Write below a list of people you can approach about this.

Reflect

and

Respond

5. Am I sensitive to what God is saying to the whole body of Christ?

It is easy to become consumed with our own little world. When we do this, we can miss what the Holy Spirit wants to teach us through the rest of the body of Christ. We can learn from each movement and deepen our understanding of both God and other Christian students. We must gain God's perspective; we need to get a "bird's eye" view at life.

Reflect and Respond...

How aware are you of what God is doing on the college campus? What can you do to stay more informed and up-to-date with God's work in the body of Christ as a whole?

Reflect

and

Respond

6. Am I over concerned with building my own "image"?

This is a motive question. We must answer it honestly. Why do we do what we do? Are we concerned more with building our image or our substance? Are we too concerned with who gets the credit or with who has the title? Do we pursue recognition or results? This will divert the best of leaders into a selfish direction.

Reflect and Respond...

Are you over-concerned with building your own "image"? Answer this honestly. How concerned are you with receiving credit or recognition for what you have done? How important is it to you to be accepted?

Reflect
    and
        Respond

7. Am I too impressed with the sensation of "signs and wonders"?

I am convinced God wants to demonstrate His power to those around us. However, it is easy to lose perspective and want our "miracle" more than we want our Maker. Jesus gave perspective on this issue with His disciples in Luke 10:17-20. Here is the acid test: when God uses you greatly, does it humble you or feed your ego?

Reflect and Respond...

Has there been a time in the past where God has done a great work through you? What happened? What was your response or reaction?

Reflect
    and
        Respond

8. Am I too independent in my life and ministry?

God desires that we grow interdependent with each other, not independent of each other. His will is always understood in the midst of community. It is dangerous to travel alone. Dr. David Cho, the pastor of the largest church in the world in Seoul, Korea, was asked why he always had someone with him when he traveled. He responded, "Because I am vulnerable to sexual temptation." He understands the danger of independence.

Reflect and Respond...

Who are you including in your ministry? Who do you have along your side to help you?

Reflect
and
Respond

Group Up

Share ways that you can position yourself to hear God.

How can you be sure you don't miss something He is trying to tell you?

9. Am I aware and honest about my weaknesses?

It is too easy to play games and pretend to be doing well. It is difficult to admit weaknesses and ask for help. Good leaders are honest. They invite others to confront them and support them in the areas of their weakness. They even ask others where they are weak, because they understand how normal it is to have blind spots in those areas. Awareness and honesty about our weaknesses is the first step toward improving them.

Reflect and Respond...

Are you aware of what your weaknesses are? What are they? What are you doing to make sure that you are listening when God is trying to reveal an area of weakness?

Reflect
and
Respond

10. Is my calling constantly before me?

This is an important question to ask ourselves. It's easy to get caught up in the day-to-day grind, and forget our calling from God. Do you remember Esau? He gave up his birthright for a single meal (Heb. 12:16)! Instead, we must imitate Paul, who reminded himself of his calling constantly. Three times in the book of Acts, Paul shared his calling with others. This kept him on track.

Reflect and Respond...

How are you keeping your calling in view? Write down at least 3 ways you keep your call in view.

1.

2.

3.

Assess Yourself

How strong is your character? After reading about what constitutes good character, in what areas are you strong and in what areas are you weak?

What will you do to cultivate character in your life?

Application

What is one step you will take as a result of this chapter? When will you take it? Who will hold you accountable? Review this chapter and think about what specifically you can do to take a step toward implementing the lessons in this session. Write out what you will do and when you will do it. Ask one person in the group to hold you accountable during the week. Be ready to share the next time you meet with your group what step you took and anything you learned or gained from it.

I Have a Dream

CAPTURING A GOD-GIVEN VISION

"Then the Lord replied: 'Write down the revelation and make it plain on tablets so that a herald may run with it. For the revelation awaits an appointed time; it speaks of the end and will not prove false. Though it linger, wait for it; it will certainly come and will not delay. '"
Habakkuk 2:2-3

Envisioning a Win

Toward the beginning of the twentieth century, the United States Olympic team crossed the Atlantic Ocean by ship to participate in the games that year. As you might imagine, the deck of the ship was a picture of activity. Athletes were preparing themselves by stretching, running, jumping, and lifting weights.

That is everyone except for Jim Thorpe, the great Native American athlete. Jim was simply sitting on a deck chair with his eyes closed. He looked like he was simply relaxing, catching some rays, before the work began. When his coach spotted him, he confronted him. "Thorpe, what do you think you're doing?"

With a smile on his face, Jim Thorpe just opened one eye and responded, "I'm watching myself win the decathlon."

Whether he knew it or not, Jim Thorpe was practicing something as powerful as a workout for athletes. He was using the power of vision—those mental images we all have on the inside of us—to move him toward his goal. Interestingly, Jim Thorpe did go on to win the decathlon that year. And his clear inward vision played a major role.

The tool of vision is not some new age idea. It is a New Testament idea. In fact, saints have tapped into the power of a God-given vision as far back as Noah and Abraham. (Heb. 11:13). We all think in pictures. If I say the word "elephant" to you, you don't picture the letters of that word, you picture a big, gray animal in your head. God designed our minds to work this way. So, when we can tap into clear pictures of a better tomorrow, those images can propel us to fulfilling that vision.

What is Vision?

All good leaders are driven by vision. They are not satisfied with maintaining the status quo. They long to take their organization somewhere. But just what is vision?

Several leaders have attempted to define vision in simple terms:
- ⬦ Vision is foresight with insight based on hindsight.
- ⬦ Vision is seeing the invisible and making it visible.
- ⬦ Vision is an informed bridge from the present to a better future.

Capturing a God-given Vision

Guided Prayer
Dear God,
give me eyes
to see the possibilities
of what You are
wanting to accomplish
in this world.

Reveal to me the vision
You have for my life.

Ignite a passion within
me for a specific work
in Your Kingdom.

Amen.

Define It

For our purposes, let me suggest the following definition for you to consider.

Vision is:

> **A clear mental image of a preferable future imparted by God to His chosen servants. It is based on the belief that it not only could be done but should be done.**

Vision is a picture held in your mind's eye of the way things could and should be in the days ahead. Vision connotes a visual reality, a portrait of a preferred future. The picture is internal and personal. Sometimes it is so personal that it is difficult to explain to others.

The famous jazz musician, Duke Ellington, was asked to define rhythm. He thought for a moment and then responded, "If you got it, you don't need no definition. If you don't, ain't no definition gonna help."[1] The same could be said when trying to define vision.

Eventually, you will have to paint this mental portrait inside others if you wish the vision to materialize in your organization. Just as you have used your imagination to create this view of the future, you will have to help others catch the same vision inside of them so that they can share in its implementation.

INGREDIENTS OF A DIVINE VISION

A divine vision will consist of the following components:

- **A Clear Mental Image**
  It serves as a sort of blueprint on the inside.
- **A Positive Change**
  It involves improving present conditions.
- **A Future Focus**
  It furnishes direction to the unseen future.
- **A Gift from God**
  It is divinely inspired, not humanly manipulated.
- **A Chosen People & Time**
  It fits a specific leader and time period.

Reflect and Respond...

What vision is in your mind that you feel God is calling you to accomplish? This does not have to be an overall vision for your life purpose. Maybe right now you simply have a vision for an immediate need in your community or campus. Write about it.

Reflect
and
Respond

Vision is a clear mental image of a preferable future imparted by God to His chosen servants. It is based on the belief that it not only could be done but should be done.

THE BIRTH OF A VISION

For most of us, the vision begins hazy, without a lot of detail. You don't know all the where's, what's, who's, or how's. More likely it's just an idea in your mind. You can identify something that you feel passionate about, something that you strongly feel should be done. You will notice that the conception and birth of a vision is much like the birth of a child. There are various stages that it goes through as it matures. John Dawson has noticed this truth and inspired the following stages.[2]

Intimacy

This is the place of beginnings. People who catch a vision do so because they have spent time with God in quietness, solitude, and reflection. Just as a husband and wife will never give birth to a baby unless they come together intimately, a person will never give birth to a vision without experiencing intimacy with God. The union of you and God provides Him the opportunity to speak to you and reveal what He wants to do.

Solitude

Are you taking time to pray and reflect? Are you experiencing intimacy with God? On a scale of 1–10 with "10" the highest, mark where you feel you are in your intimacy with God.

```
|----|----|----|----|----|----|----|----|----|----|
1    2    3    4    5    6    7    8    9    10
```

Conception

God may not communicate a vision every time you meet, in the same way that every time a husband and wife come together, the woman doesn't become pregnant. However, when God does reveal His vision for you, it comes in seed form and must grow inside of you. It may still be fuzzy without all of the details, but it is real and forming inside. When God is the source of your vision, one characteristic is always present. Just like a baby looks a lot like mom and a lot like dad, this vision will resemble both you and God. It fits your passion and gifts, and it will be so big that it requires God to pull it off.

Conception

Has God revealed anything like this to you yet? What is He saying to you?

Gestation

This period of time is often the longest stage of the process. During this time the leader identifies with the problem, intercedes for the people, and intervenes in the process. When we identify with the problem, we feel compassion and are burdened by it. When we intercede for the people, we labor in prayer, asking God to fulfill His vision in them and meet their needs. When we intervene in the process, we get involved in seeing the vision realized. One more thing. When a baby is growing on the inside of a mother, it changes the mother dramatically. The same is true about a vision growing inside of you.

Gestation

What stage of the gestation process are you in? Do you identify with a problem? How are you praying for that need?

Labor

This stage is often the most painful. Just as a woman's birth pains increase in intensity and frequency, so the fight intensifies just before the vision is fulfilled. The enemy would like nothing more than for you to abort the vision before it comes to pass. So, your toughest moments will likely come just before you give birth to it! Hang on. Look for your struggles to become deeper and more numerous. Don't give up. Labor is a good sign that something is about to happen!

Have you ever experienced this? Do you anticipate this stage soon in your leadership? Do you know students who are at this stage and are spiritual leaders on the campus? What is one thing you can do to help with the "labor"?

Group Up

Share as a group where each of you are in this process.

Birth

Finally, the vision is born. All that has been going on inside the heart of the leader is ultimately realized. Everyone can now see the fruit of the prayer, planning, and work. And just like giving birth to a baby, you feel the vision God gave you is the most beautiful one of all! You feel a special affinity to it and you want to protect it. This is very natural. But now you have to let it grow up. Eventually, you must let it stand on its own. Celebrate this process, just like you would a child.

Have you seen a vision fulfilled while on campus? What visions have you celebrated in the past?

Real Life

I love the story of Charles Darrow. He had a vision in the 1920s of becoming a millionaire. In fact, he married his wife on the premise that they would be rich within ten years. Unfortunately, the stock market crashed in 1929 and the Great Depression began. Charles and his wife lost almost everything: their savings, their cars, their jobs. They even had to mortgage their home. In 1932, Charles admitted to his wife that he was a failure. They obviously were never going to become millionaires. He told her if she wanted to leave him it would be alright with him. Fortunately, she was also a person with vision. She told him she had not given up on their dream. She felt they should simply do something every day to keep the dream alive until they saw it fulfilled. She suggested they sit down after dinner each night and talk about what they would do if they had a million dollars. This began a discipline for them. They faithfully did this each night for months. Then, when the exercise became a bit dull, they added new dimensions to it. They created play money and divided it up. They would exchange it back and forth like they were consumers and bankers. Later, they created little houses, hotels and a game board.

Does this sound familiar? You guessed it. Charles Darrow and his wife had just invented a game many of us own today. The game of Monopoly. What's more, three years later, in 1935, Parker Brothers bought that game from Mr. Darrow. Do you know how much money they gave him for it? One million dollars! That's the power of keeping the dream alive, even in tough times. How much more should we, who are connected to God and an eternal vision, keep our vision alive?

COMMON QUALITIES

While every vision will be as unique and varied as each person who is born, there will be common traits that every leader's vision shares.

- It is unique and personal.
- It is larger than mere ideas or preferences.
- It requires the leader to act as an innovator.
- It is an inward image that is both conceptual and practical.

Whose Vision is It?

As leaders called by God to accomplish His work in this world, ultimately it should be our goal to carry out a vision that is from God, not ourselves. Unfortunately, it can be all too easy to begin pursuing our own agenda, rather than one divinely inspired. Here is how you can determine whose vision you are carrying – your own or one from God.

Man-made Vision	God-given Vision
• You create it based on your gifts and skills.	• You receive it as a revelation from God.
• Its fulfillment rests on staying ahead of others.	• Its fulfillment rests on the person's obedience.
• Other similar organizations are seen as competitors.	• Other similar organizations are seen as complimentary.
• Its goal is to build your organization and generate revenue.	• Its goal is to serve people, advance God's rule, and to honor God.
• Stress may emerge both inwardly and outwardly.	• It is accompanied by inward peace and outward opposition.
• It may be dropped for something better.	• It is compelling and captivating until fulfilled.

Two Visions, One God-given

When I became a youth pastor in college, I had a vision to reach high school students in the city. One of my early attempts, however, was a miserable failure. I got a vision for starting a Christian movie cinema in town. There was an old building for rent. I raised the money to lease it and soon began renovation. I recruited workers to help hammer nails and paint. The first three months were exciting. Then, it became hard. The money slowed down. The volunteers were busy. Soon, I ran out of gas emotionally and spiritually. The idea never came to pass.

Interestingly, my burden for reaching students had not died. I waited on God for new direction. Within a year, I took a whole new road to accomplishing my vision. I began to develop a multi-media presentation that could be shown in public high schools. Soon, I trained my students in how to share the vision with their teachers and to ask if they could sponsor it in the school. I had a team working on the production. It was excellent. Schools began to say yes. Eventually, we all gave birth to the vision. The presentation gave Christian students a platform to share their faith. That production enabled our youth group to share Christ with one out of every five students in the city.

One vision worked. The other didn't. Both seemed like good ideas, but clearly, the second one was a God-given vision. I worshiped. I watched. I waited. Then I worked.

Steps to Fulfilling God's Vision

Matthew 9:35-10:8 marks a pivotal point in Jesus' ministry. Up until this point, Jesus was doing the ministry with His disciples watching. Read this passage and observe the process that takes place and the strategy Jesus adopts as He goes about fulfilling His God-given vision.

☺ **Get active in service and initiate obedience.**
"Jesus went through all the towns and villages" (9:35a).

Jesus did not lounge around by the sea of Galilee waiting for ministry opportunities to come to Him. He was out and about, talking with people and entering into their lives. He was actively serving and meeting people where they were at.

☺ **Communicate the revelation you have already.**
"Teaching in their synagogues, preaching the good news of the kingdom" (9:35b)

Do you realize that you already know 95% of God's will? "How?" you may ask. "I feel like I am constantly trying to figure out His will for my life." Open your Bible. God has revealed 95% of His will for our lives there, yet we constantly badger Him for the other 5%, like our mate, our career or our future. God simply says, Obey what you already know, then I will show you more.

☺ **Observe and understand the reality of human conditions.**
"When he saw the crowds" (9:36a).

Jesus was there among the people watching them. He saw the pained expressions on their faces and the physical aliments that afflicted them as they came to Him for healing. He stopped long enough to observe and understand their condition.

☉ Allow God to burden you with a specific need.

"He had compassion on them, because they were harassed and helpless, like sheep without a shepherd" (9:36b).

Jesus' heart was moved. He felt pity for them and the condition they were in. This is how every vision begins: with a burden. You see something wrong, something that is not being done that should be done. From this a vision is born. When a heart is stirred by a need, that is when God imparts a vision to meet that need.

☉ Seek a divine diagnosis: What is the issue to be resolved?

"'The harvest is plentiful, but the workers are few" (9:37).

Jesus saw the need: the people needed physical, emotional and spiritual healing. And then He identified the problem: there were not enough people to bring them the message of hope and healing. Jesus had been doing the work of healing by Himself up until this point. But there were more people with needs than He was able to touch. His diagnosis: big harvest, few workers.

☉ Pray to determine what action could meet that need.

"'Ask the Lord of the harvest, therefore, to send out workers into his harvest field'" (9:38).

So what did Jesus determine would meet that need? More workers! And that's what He prayed for. Notice that He didn't pray for better choirs, bigger buildings, or more money. The one action He prayed for was that God send out more workers.

☉ Choose a team and empower them for partnership.

"He called his twelve disciples to him and gave them authority" (10:1).

Without a vision, the people perish. However, there is another truth we must grasp. Without people, a vision perishes. Jesus was not able to care for the needs of the people on His own. That was the problem. He needed more workers to join Him, to help Him fulfill His vision. So He formed a team and empowered them to help Him.

☉ Take immediate action toward the fulfillment of the vision.

"These twelve Jesus sent out" (10:5).

Jesus doesn't hesitate a bit. He chooses a team and immediately sends them out with instructions on how to carry out His work. He imparts the vision and equips them with the tools to fulfill it. They become the answer to His prayer request for workers.

Reflect and Respond...

What strikes you about the process that Jesus goes through to fulfill His God-given vision?

Group Up

Share the insights you have gained from your study of how Jesus fulfilled His God-given vision.

Do you identify with any of the eight steps outlined from Matthew 9:35-10:8? These are steps to fulfilling God's vision. Are you anywhere along that process? List the eight from memory. Indicate where you are in the process.

Reflect **Steps**   **Process**

and

Respond

1.

2.

3.

4.

5.

6.

7.

8.

Real Life

The vision of a theme park was his. He told those who worked with him that he knew who he wanted to oversee the building up of his theme park. He wanted the man who put the U.S. Navy back in the Pacific Ocean after the bombing of Pearl Harbor. The man was Admiral Joe Fowler. But when the owner approached him, Fowler responded by saying: "You don't understand. I'm retired. I'm through." But the owner wouldn't give up. After sharing the details of his vision, Joe agreed. Years later it was time to build another park. Can you guess who the theme park people approached to build it? They went to Joe Fowler again, at age 77. He said, "You don't understand. I'm retired. I'm through." But when they shared the vision in detail, he came out of retirement the second time and took the job. Finally, in the 80s, the theme park was finished. The owner had gone again to Joe Fowler, who was 87 years old! When he reminded them he was retired, it didn't slow them down at all. They shared the vision, he caught it, and supervised the building. His favorite phrase, "You don't understand. I'm retired. I'm through." soon changed to, "You don't have to die until you want to!" That's the power of a vision!

How Visions Unfold

In 1886, Dr. John Pemberton had begun selling his elixir. It was a smashing success. He claimed it calmed nerves and reduced headache pain. He only hoped drugstores would stock it in greater quantities as its popularity increased. Little did he know what it was destined to become. One afternoon, a drug store clerk accidentally mixed it with carbonated water instead of tap water. Instantly, a whole new vision for this elixir was born. It was so refreshing!

In 1888, Dr. Pemberton's bubbly elixir was first called "Coca Cola." That's when Asa Candler came along with a much bigger vision for it. Candler thought it would be better sold as a soft drink, from a fountain, to refresh shoppers. He bought the formula from Pemberton and sold it to drugstores in big red barrels. The elixir took off as a thirst quencher, but was still sold only in drug stores. That is until two men came along with an even bigger vision for it. Mr. Thomas and Mr. Whitehead approached Candler with a vision for selling "Coke" in bottles, both in the drug store and in grocers across the country. Candler didn't share the vision. He thought it would never work. So, he sold the idea to the two gentlemen for $1. Soon Coke was offered in a whole new fashion. In 1916, the contour bottle was patented and the drink was consumed all over the U.S.

That is when a man named Woodruff came along with an even bigger vision for it. He believed it would sell big all over the world! In 1919, Candler was talked into selling out of the business, and Woodruff took it internationally. Today, the taste of Coke is on the lips of people in almost every country of the world (on your campus?). Very often this is how a vision unfolds. It begins with a person and an idea. Then others may come along who see even bigger possibilities. They take the vision to a whole new level. God can use a variety of people to accomplish His great plans.

Three Word Pictures

We have been focusing on the internal, personal aspect of forming and clarifying a vision, but if a vision is ever going to be materialized, it must go beyond that. It needs to be shared with others. To be a leader you not only must conceive the vision, you must cast the vision.

As a vision-caster, you will want to incarnate these analogies for your people:
- **Artist**
  You are painting pictures inside of the people who hear you.
- **Prophet**
  You are prophetically speaking words of conviction about the future.
- **Lobbyist**
  You are representing a cause, compelling people to join you in the effort.

Reflect and Respond...

Think practically about how to cast vision as an artist, prophet, and lobbyist. What do these roles look like to you? Which ones have you performed? How?

Reflect

and

Respond

Group Up

Discuss the word pictures given on this page.

What do these look like in practical terms in relation to casting a vision?

Casting the Vision

Once the vision has developed in your own mind, the next step is to share the vision with others. You will need to help others see a vision of the future that you see. Examine one of God's visions for your life in Jeremiah 29:11. Here are twelve key factors you will need to take into consideration as you bring others on board and attempt to communicate your vision.

1. Embrace and own the vision yourself.
For others to catch the vision and embrace it, you first need to embrace the vision yourself. This seems obvious, doesn't it? Why would others invest in a vision that their leader first is not completely sold on? You need to believe whole-heartedly in the importance and value of the vision, making it your own. Here are several ways to determine whether you have done this. Does the vision involve your:

⬥ Natural talents – What do you naturally do well?
⬥ Spiritual gifts – What has God gifted you to do?
⬥ Inward desires – What do you want to do?
⬥ Results and fruit – What produces the most fruit when you do it?
⬥ Affirmation and recognition – What do others confirm about you?
⬥ Burdens and passion – What convictions do you feel compelled to pursue?
⬥ Fulfillment and satisfaction – What do you deeply enjoy doing?
⬥ Circumstances and opportunities – What is in front of you as an opportunity?

2. Engage the soul of the people.
The ancient Chinese spoke of the "will" as being like a cart that is pulled by two horses: the "mind" and the "emotions". Both horses need to be moving in the same direction to pull the cart forward. In order to bring people into the vision, we must speak to both the mind and emotions. You cannot just try to convince people of the importance of the vision, you must speak to their hearts and stir their souls.

3. Speak to their needs.
If your vision does not touch a need in their life, people will not see the importance of it for their life. You need to understand the people and know the keys to their heart.

⬥ What do they cry about?   ⬥ What do they laugh about?
⬥ What do they sing about?   ⬥ What do they plan about?
⬥ What do they dream about?   ⬥ What do they talk about?

If you know these things, you know the things that move the heart of the people. If your vision speaks to these, then it will motivate the people.

4. Paint pictures on the inside of them.
People think and remember in pictures. Images fill their minds as they watch TV, the movies, or even log onto the Internet. In order to drive your vision home, nearly everyone needs a POINT for their head, and a PICTURE for their heart.

5. Provide application not merely information.
We must furnish something to do, not just think about. People need tangible action steps they can take if they're going to "own" the vision themselves.

In order to bring people into the vision, we must speak to both the mind and emotions. You cannot just try to convince people of the importance of the vision, you must speak to their hearts and stir their souls.

6. Communicate the benefits of buying into the vision.

Most people are tuned into W.I.I.F.M. radio: What's In It For Me? They rarely do anything until they see the personal, measurable benefits of taking action. John Maxwell believes most people don't change until they…

KNOW enough that they are able to,
CARE enough that they want to,
HURT enough that they have to.

7. Enlarge their world.

People want to be a part of something bigger than themselves. Let them see how they can leave a legacy behind them by participating in the vision.

8. Model personal commitment and call for it from others.

The number one motivational principle is this: People do what people see. They rarely follow mere talk. They will watch the one who is casting the vision to see just how committed they are to the big idea before jumping in themselves. We need to follow the sequence illustrated in Ezra 7:10, "For Ezra had devoted himself to the study and observance of the Law of the Lord, and to teaching its decrees and laws in Israel."

9. Allow time for acceptance.

Marketing experts and salesmen tell us that people generally need to hear an idea seven times before they will embrace it and call it their own idea. And the time necessary for this ownership varies.

⋄ Approximately 10% of our population are "pioneers".
⋄ About 70% of the population are "settlers".
⋄ Then, about 20% are "antagonists", who may never jump on board with the vision.

The group you must win over is the "settlers".

10. Create an atmosphere.

Good leaders and visionaries create a sense of destiny, a sense of family, and a militant spirit in the people who listen to them. Cultivating an atmosphere is essential to creating a "critical mass" in your constituency. High morale, positive peer pressure, and forward momentum are a leader's best friends.

11. Employ a variety of people to help cast the vision in a trickle down process.

One person cannot "connect" with everybody. The leader responsible for communicating the vision should employ a variety of others who compliment him or her and who can say it in a fresh way to those with a different style and temperament. The vision is disseminated best when the leader shares it with the staff; the staff with their key volunteers; the key volunteers with those in their sphere of influence, and they eventually will connect with the others. The "buy in" should come from the top.

12. Demonstrate passion.

Passion begets passion. We don't attract who we want to the vision – we attract who we are. We must demonstrate passion and communicate enough credibility to make them want to follow the vision.

High morale, positive peer pressure, and forward momentum are a leader's best friends.

Group Up

Discuss with the group which of these twelve key factors come most naturally to you and which are difficult for you.

HOW WE MUST HANDLE VISION...

See it Clearly

Show it Creatively

Say it Constantly

Assess Yourself...

A vision is:

_____

_____

_____

Where are you in the process of capturing a God-given vision? Review the stages of the birth of a vision and reflect on what stage you are experiencing.

What can you do to encourage the growth of this vision? What needs to happen to take you to the next stage?

What do you think you will struggle with as a vision-caster?

Guided Prayer

Heavenly Father,
I believe You have
a great work for my
life as a servant of
Your Kingdom.

Impart to me a vision
for this work.

Begin to paint a picture
in my mind and place
a burden upon my
heart for whatever it
is You desire me to do.

May I watch, wait,
and at the right
time go to work
fulfilling this vision.

Amen.

Application

You may not have your life vision yet - the big picture view of what God's main purpose for your life is - but think about what burdens are on your heart where you are now. What smaller scale visions might you be able to fulfill? Search your heart and pray over what God may be calling you to accomplish at this time in your life. Choose one idea that you believe may be a God-given vision. Write it down. To keep this vision alive and fresh in your mind, post photos, pictures, and quotes that represent your goals and dreams in a place where you will see it often. Remember that God wants to accomplish great things through you right now where you are!

The Art of the Basin and the Towel

THE MARKS OF A SERVANT LEADER

"Jesus called them together and said, 'You know that the rulers of the Gentiles lord it over them, and their high officials exercise authority over them. Not so with you. Instead, whoever wants to become great among you must be your servant, and whoever wants to be first must be your slave – just as the Son of Man did not come to be served, but to serve, and to give his life as a ransom for many.'"

Matthew 20:25-28

Satisfying Every Customer

In December of 2000, Chick-Fil-A restaurants reached a milestone. They surpassed a billion dollars in sales. This was especially meaningful due to the fact that they remain closed on Sunday, which is the top sales day of the week for retailers. They do so to allow employees a chance to be in worship and with family.

The story of Chick-Fil-A is a story of servant leadership. From the beginning, Truett Cathy determined he would run his business based on biblical principles. They would always be closed on Sundays. The staff at headquarters would serve the stores, which would, in turn, serve the customers. Each year, the operators are invited to come to a conference to equip them to lead more effectively. All expenses are paid. They are served there by the team at headquarters.

A friend of mine, David Salyers, is vice president of marketing at Chick-Fil-A. He told me that the senior staff is committed to servant leadership. Each month, they take turns handling the complaint calls that come in. They give away hundreds of thousands of dollars to worthwhile causes. They even scholarship student employees to go to college.

On a road trip, David told me he traveled with Dan Cathy, executive under his dad, the founder. That night, David mentioned to Dan that he wished someone would invent luggage that wouldn't wrinkle his shirts when he traveled. It was simply a passing comment before he went to bed. In the morning, David discovered that Dan had gotten his shirts and was trying to iron them all before he awoke.

Is it any wonder why their average store outsells the other leading fast food chains? All of us are attracted to leaders and organizations that are committed to genuine service.

Basic Truth
The goal of healthy leadership is to serve people.

Guided Prayer
Father, I desire to be a leader devoted to serving You in all I do.

Reveal to me what it means to be a Christ-like servant leader.

Empty me of myself and my ideas on how to lead, and fill me with Your truth.

Amen.

TEMPTATIONS OF LEADERSHIP

This issue of servant leadership poses the single greatest contrast between spiritual and secular leadership. During His three and a half year ministry, Jesus consistently taught His disciples that leadership meant servanthood - as opposed to the "top down" attitude the Gentiles demonstrated during that day (Matt. 20:25-28).

In his book, *In the Name of Jesus*,[1] Henri Nouwen mentions three very real yet subtle temptations that any servant of Christ faces. They correspond with the three temptations our Lord faced before He began His earthly ministry.

First Temptation: To be Self-Sufficient

Jesus' first temptation was to turn stones into bread. It probably would not make our top ten list of sins. However, it would have meant acting apart from His Father in heaven. He would have assumed the role of meeting His own needs.

This attitude stands in direct opposition to everything we know about the Kingdom. As leaders, we must continue to foster our dependence on the Lord. Instead of being self-assured, we need to be open, unguarded, and vulnerable.

Second Temptation: To be Spectacular

Jesus' second temptation was to jump off the pinnacle of the Temple. After all, the angels would catch Him. What a gimmick! It would have attracted all kinds of attention. It would have made people sit up and take notice. His popularity would have soared. But Jesus refused.

Paul says this is to be deliberately renounced, as Jesus renounced it. In Nouwen's words, "Jesus refused to be a stunt man… He did not come to walk on hot coals, swallow fires or put His hand in a lion's mouth to demonstrate He had something worthwhile to say."[2]

Third Temptation: To be Powerful

Jesus' third temptation was tough. Satan promised to give Him all the kingdoms of the world if He would just bow down and worship him. Jesus could have have bypassed the cross and become an all-powerful leader overnight. This would have been a shortcut.

Paul's comment is superb: "For we do not preach ourselves, but Jesus Christ as Lord, and ourselves as your servants for Jesus' sake" (2 Cor. 4:5). Paul even confessed that he came to the Corinthians in weakness, not in strength, that their faith should not rest in the power of men, but in the power of God. To lead is appropriate, necessary, and good. But to push, to manipulate, and to be in full control is never right. Put simply, one God is sufficient!

Group Up

Share ways in which a leader can resist these temptations.

Refer to the way Jesus handled temptation when he was faced with it in Matthew 4:1-11, and Luke 4:1-13.

Reflect and Respond...

Which of these three temptation(s) are you most vulnerable to as a leader?

Reflect

In what ways can you resist these temptations? (Look at the model Jesus gives for overcoming temptation in Matt. 4:1-11 and Luke 4:1-13.) Jot down several ways you can resist temptations.

and

1.

2.

Respond

3.

4.

5.

Horizontal Thinking vs. Vertical Thinking

On a regular basis, Jesus guided his disciples away from "horizontal thinking" and steered them toward "vertical thinking". Far too often, they started looking at each other and comparing what they had done with what others had done. Once in a while they worried if they were receiving enough credit or getting enough prestige. This is evident even at the last supper.

"Within minutes they were bickering over who of them would end up the greatest. But Jesus intervened: 'Kings like to throw their weight around and people in authority like to give themselves fancy titles. It's not going to be that way with you. Let the senior among you become like the junior; let the leader act the part of the servant'" (Luke 22: 24-26, The Message).

Notice that Jesus did not rebuke them for their desire to be great, he just gave them an unexpected formula on what constitutes greatness. Jesus once again tries to shift their thinking. Only when you adopt "vertical thinking" does the statement "the first shall be last and last shall be first" make any sense.

Group Up

As a group discuss in more detail the difference between "horizontal thinking" and "vertical thinking."

What other passage in Scripture can you find where Jesus tries to communicate this point?

PRACTICING THE ART OF THE BASIN AND THE TOWEL: JOHN 13:1-20

In this passage Jesus demonstrates through action what He has been trying to communicate through His words on servant leadership. He lives out His words, "Let the senior among you become like a junior; let the leader act the part of the servant." Jesus shows us what it means to be a Christ-like servant leader.

1. Christlike Leaders are Motivated by LOVE to Serve Others.

"Just before the Passover Feast, Jesus knew that the time had come to leave this world to go to the Father. Having loved his dear companions, he continued to love them right to the end. It was suppertime. The devil by now had Judas, son of Simon Iscariot, firmly in his grip..." (John 13:1-2, The Message)

Love

This may sound obvious, but servant leadership cannot be artificially contrived. It must be motivated by love. Authentic love. Not duty. Not obligation. Not profit. Not popularity among the people. Love is the only motive strong enough to keep a leader washing feet. Jesus' love was...

- ◦ possessive
- ◦ continuous
- ◦ unconditional
- ◦ unselfish

"Everybody can be great...because anybody can serve. You don't have to have a college degree to serve. You don't have to make your subject and verb agree to serve. You only need a heart full of grace. A soul generated by love." Dr. Martin Luther King, Jr.

Love is Able

A wealthy visitor walked by Mother Teresa in Calcutta, India. She was caring for a leper whose skin was badly peeling and bleeding. The odor was strong and the sight was unappealing. The man looked down and scoffed: "How can you do that? I'm telling you, I wouldn't do that for a million dollars!"

Mother Teresa just looked up with a smile and replied, "Neither would I."

What money could never get her to do, love was able.

Reflect and Respond...

What is driving you to serve others? Honestly evaluate your motives.

Reflect and Respond

How can you ensure that love remains the only motive driving you to serve? One of the CrossSeeker principles is "service." Thousands of college students use their spring break to serve others. Why do you feel they would make this choice?

2. Christlike Leaders Possess a SECURITY that Allows Them to Minister to Others.

"Jesus knew that the Father had put him in charge of everything; that he came from God and was on his way back to God..." (John 13:3, The Message).

Jesus was a secure leader. His security came from three things He knew to be true:
- ◇ Jesus knew His POSITION and was willing to not flaunt it.
- ◇ Jesus knew His CALLING and was willing to be faithful to it.
- ◇ Jesus knew His FUTURE and was willing to submit to it.

Only those who are secure will be able to do great things... and small things. Security is the prerequisite to great undertakings. Only the secure will STRETCH. Security is also the prerequisite to small undertakings. Only the secure will STOOP. Servanthood begins with security! The secure are into towels. The insecure are into titles. The secure are people conscious. The insecure are position conscious. The secure want to add value to others. The insecure want to receive value from others.

Real Life

Abraham Lincoln was probably the most criticized President in history. Folks in the South were brutal because of his stance on slavery. Many in the north made fun of his looks. Even some of his own staff were cruel to him. Secretary of State Stanton called him an ape. This might have driven Lincoln out of office had it not been for his keen sense of identity and security.

On one occasion, one of his Generals told him how another Union officer had blasted at him, calling him names and criticizing his policies. Afterward, the general asked what Lincoln thought of him. The President smiled and said he thought he was a marvelous leader. The general couldn't believe his ears. "Mr. President! Didn't you hear what I just told you this officer said about you?"

"Yes, I heard you," Lincoln responded. "But you see – you just asked me what I thought of him, not what he thought of me."[3]

Reflect and Respond...

How secure are you as a leader? In what areas do you need to grow to become more secure? What things do you need to know and accept to be true about yourself and God?

Security

The secure are into towels. The insecure are into titles.

The secure are people conscious. The insecure are position conscious.

The secure want to add value to others. The insecure want to receive value from others.

Group Up
Explore the reasons security is so important in leadership.

Reflect and Respond

3. Christlike Leaders INITIATE Servant Ministry to Others

"So he got up from the table, set aside his robe, and put on an apron. Then he poured water into a basin and began to wash the feet of the disciples, drying them with his apron" (John 13:4-5, The Message).

Initiate

Someone forgot to book the servant that night, and no one but Jesus volunteered for the job! Servant leaders will initiate when they see an opportunity for ministry. Note the difference between Pilate, in Matthew 27:24, and Jesus in the passage above. Jesus picked up the basin, and assumed responsibility. He put others first. Pilate picked up the basin also, but he avoided responsibility. He put himself first.

Note Jesus' attitude that allowed Him to do this:
- **He had nothing to prove.**
  Jesus didn't have to play games, project His self worth or prove Himself to anyone.
- **He had nothing to lose.**
  Jesus didn't have to guard His reputation or fear He'd lose popularity. He took risks.
- **He had nothing to hide.**
  Jesus didn't keep up a facade or image for anyone. He was vulnerable and transparent.

Customer Service Is Our Standard

A letter by a lady in hotel management related to Guest Programs. In it she details how one employee picked up the basin and assumed responsibility by going above and beyond the call of duty, putting others first.

"Not too long ago, a guest checking out of our hotel was asked how she enjoyed her visit. She told the front-desk clerk she had had a wonderful vacation, but was heartbroken about losing several rolls of Kodak color film she had not yet developed. She was particularly upset over the loss of the pictures she had shot at one of the shows, as this was a memory she especially treasured.

Now please understand that we have no written service standards covering lost snapshots. Fortunately, the hostess at the front-desk understood our hotel's philosophy of caring for our guests. She asked the woman to leave her a couple of rolls of fresh film, promising she would take care of the rest.

Two weeks later, this guest received a package at her home. In it were photos of the entire cast of our show, personally autographed by each performer. There were also photos of the fireworks in the theme park, taken by the front-desk hostess on her own time, after work. I happen to know this story because this guest wrote us a letter. She said that never in her life had she received such compassionate service from any business establishment.

Heroic service does not come from policy manuals. It comes from people who care - and from a culture that encourages and models that attitude."

Reflect and Respond...

Do you find it hard or easy to initiate servant ministry to others? Do you easily pick up the basin when an opportunity presents itself as Jesus did?

Reflect

and

Respond

Why or why not? Share at least two responses to the opportunity based on your walk with Christ. What would you do?

1.

2.

4. Christlike Leaders RECEIVE Servant Ministry from Others.

"When he got to Simon Peter, Peter said, 'Master, you wash my feet?' Jesus answered, 'You don't understand now what I'm doing, but it will be clear enough to you later.' Peter then persisted, 'You're not going to wash my feet – ever!'" (John 13:6-7, The Message).

Receive

Peter was still position conscious at this point. This is what kept him from receiving from Jesus. True servants can receive ministry as well as give it because they understand God's grace is what improves all service. They never want to stand in the way of "grace-giving."

Reflect and Respond...

How do you respond to being served? Do you receive service as freely as you give it? Or do you respond more like Peter? Why do you think this is? Jot your ideas in this space and in the sidebar if necessary.

Reflect

and

Respond

5. Christlike Leaders Want Nothing to Interfere with their RELATIONSHIP with Jesus.

"Jesus said, 'If I don't wash you, you can't be a part of what I'm doing.' 'Master!' said Peter. 'Not only my feet, then. Wash my hands! Wash my head!'" (John 13:8-9, The Message).

Relationship

Peter moves from one extreme to the other. Why? He hungered to be rightly related to Jesus. Once he realized it was okay for Jesus to wash him – he wanted an entire bath! He did everything with reckless abandon. It is love for God, as well as love for people, that is behind a servant leader's behavior. They respond quickly to God's connection in their lives.

Group Up

Discuss the reasons why it might be hard for a leader to receive servant ministry.

What gets in the way of your relationship with Jesus?

Reflect

Do you approach your relationship with God with the same reckless abandon that Peter shows in this passage? If not, how can you begin freeing yourself up to do so?

and

Respond

6. Christlike Leaders Teach Servanthood by Their EXAMPLE.

"After he had finished washing their feet, he took his robe, put it back on and went back to his place at the table. Then he said, 'Do you understand what I have done to you? You address me as Teacher and Master, and rightly so. This is what I am. So if I, the Master and Teacher, washed your feet, then you must now wash each other's feet. I've laid a pattern for you'" (John 13:12-15, The Message).

Example

Jesus could have sat at the table that night and given them a good sermon on servanthood, or scolded them for not booking the servant to be at the door. Instead, He decided to make an object lesson out of it. He knew words would not be enough.

Leaders cannot lecture people into serving others. If lectures or sermons were enough, we would have changed the world long ago. Leaders who get organizations to serve, model it for their people. When it starts at the top, it always trickles down. What a leader does always get emulated, good or bad.

As stated before, the number one motivational principle is: People do what people see! If you model servant leadership, others will naturally learn by your example.

Real Life

Progressive Auto Insurance understands this servanthood principle. They have begun to place company vans on the roadways, primed for a chance to serve their customers if they get into an accident.

When they get a call, the closest one rushes to the scene. Upon arrival, they make sure everyone is okay. Once they confirm this, they help their customer into the van, and serve them coffee and snacks. On the spot they make calls to the appropriate authorities. Then, they begin to adjust the claim, right there on the spot! In 90% of their cases, the customer walks away with a check covering the damages to their car.

These claim adjusters have to carry lots of business cards with them, however. Most of the time, the OTHER driver asks for a card. They are so impressed with the service, they decide they are going to change companies!

What type of servanthood are you modeling right now?

Reflect

and

Respond

7. Christlike Leaders Live a BLESSED Life.

"What I've done, you do. I'm only pointing out the obvious. A servant is not ranked above his master; an employee doesn't give orders to the employer. If you understand what I'm telling you, act like it – and live a blessed life" (John 13:16-17, The Message).

Blessed

Dr. Albert Schweitzer, theologian and medical missionary, once said, "I don't know what your destiny will be, but one thing I know: the only ones among you who will be really happy are those who will have sought and found out how to serve." The truth is that when we serve others, we are blessed in return.

HOW DO WE LIVE A BLESSED LIFE?

When Jesus saw His ministry drawing huge crowds, He climbed the hillside. Those who were apprenticed to Him, the committed, climbed with Him. Arriving at a quiet place, He sat down and taught His climbing companions. This is what He said:

⋄ You're blessed when you're at the end of your rope. With less of you there is more of God and his rule.

⋄ You're blessed when you feel you've lost what is most dear to you. Only then can you be embraced by the One most dear to you.

⋄ You're blessed when you're content with just who you are – no more, no less. That's the moment you find yourselves proud owners of everything that can't be bought.

⋄ You're blessed when you've worked up a good appetite for God. He's food and drink in the best meal you'll ever eat.

⋄ You're blessed when you care. At the moment of being 'care-full,' you find yourselves cared for.

⋄ You're blessed when you get your inside world – your mind and heart put right. Then you can see God in the outside world.

⋄ You're blessed when you can show people how to cooperate instead of compete or fight. That's when you discover who you really are, and your place in God's family.

⋄ You're blessed when your commitment to God provokes persecution. The persecution drives you even deeper into God's Kingdom.

Matthew 5:1-10 (The Message)

"I don't know what your destiny will be, but one thing I know: the only ones among you who will be really happy are those who will have sought and found out how to serve."

Dr. Albert Schweitzer

The Beatitudes in the Form of Personal Disciplines:

⋄ Intentionally admit your need for God (Matt. 5:3).

⋄ Be a person of brokenness before the Lord (Matt. 5:4).

⋄ Maintain a hunger and thirst for God (Matt. 5:6).

⋄ Practice an identity with people in need (Matt. 5:7).

⋄ Maintain a pure heart (Matt. 5:8).

⋄ Cultivate peace in all relationships (Matt. 5:9).

⋄ Take a positive view of criticism (Matt. 5:10).

Reflect and Respond...

Can you think of a time when you were blessed by serving someone else?

Reflect

List three or more ways you experienced a blessing.

1.

and

2.

3. Respond

What will you do this week to implement two of the personal disciplines listed above?

8. Christlike Leaders Live their Lives OPPOSITE the Philosophy of the World.

"I'm not including all of you in this. I know precisely whom I've selected, so as not to interfere with the fulfillment of this scripture: 'The one who at bread ate my table, turned his heel against me.'" (John 13:18, The Message).

This is the paradox we as Christians live with: the ways of God are opposite of the ways of the world. Philippians 2:3-4 shows just how different Christian philosophy is from secular philosophy: "Don't push your way to the front; don't sweet talk your way to the top. Put yourself aside, and help others get ahead. Don't be obsessed with getting your own advantage. Forget yourselves long enough to lend a helping hand" (The Message).

Bible Paradoxes

God's ways are inside out and upside down from the ways of the world. In living a Christ-like life, we live our lives in contradiction to the way the world tells us to live. God's standards and values are completely opposite the world's. Note the paradoxes given in Scripture.

If I Want To...	I Must...	Scripture Reference
Save my life.	Lose my life.	Luke 9:24–26
Be lifted up.	Humble myself.	James 4:7
Be the greatest.	Be a servant.	Matthew 20:20–22
Be first.	Be last.	Matthew 19:30
Rule.	Serve...	Luke 22:26–27
Live.	Put to death the flesh.	Romans 8:23
Be strong.	Be weak.	2 Corinthians 11:30
Inherit the Kingdom.	Be poor in spirit.	Matthew 5:3
Reproduce.	Die.	John 12:24

Reflect and Respond...

Why is living this way so difficult? Share with another Christian what makes it hard to live your life opposite of the world's philosophy?

Reflect

and

Think about what could you do to start a habit of living your life opposite of the current trends?

Respond

The Paths to Power

Before we close this chapter, let's examine the way people gain power with others. Have you ever stopped to consider how leaders get power? The means by which we influence others has a lot do to with our philosophy and the pressure we feel in our lives. When we are under much pressure, we tend to give in and do whatever it takes to get the job done, even when it means using people.

Note the following list of seven paths to power. I have listed them from best to worst. Examine yourself as well as other leaders you have served under. What is the path you take most often?

1. HONOR
People follow because...
 ◇ the leader honors them by serving them.
 ◇ there is mutual respect and mutual dignity shared by the follower and leader.
 ◇ they believe in the leader and where he or she is going; they share common values.

This is the highest and longest lasting leadership. Jesus shows us that when someone leads in this way, they experience fierce loyalty and commitment from followers.

2. MOTIVATION
People follow because...
 ◇ the leader creates excitement in them to follow.
 ◇ they feel moved to action by the passion of the cause or the leader.
 ◇ they willingly go where they would not have gone themselves.

This is an even better method, where the leader moves the follower by an act of the will.

3. PERSUASION
People follow because...
 ◇ they are moved to cooperation.
 ◇ they eventually agree because of the ideas or incentives the leader furnishes.
 ◇ they are moved "through sweetness" (the meaning of the word persuasion).

This method now utilizes verbal expression that makes the person want to follow.

4. EXCHANGE
People follow because...
 ◇ the leader can do something for them.
 ◇ they want something as a provision for themselves.
 ◇ they value the position they'll have if they submit and obey.

This method is better, but still temporal. It works until one of them finds a better deal.

5. MANIPULATION

People follow because…
- ◊ they are coerced into it.
- ◊ they are verbally backed into a corner and feel they have no choice.
- ◊ they were tricked into it – they feel used and degraded.

This method is used by people who tend to be both cunning and selfish. No one stays long in this unhealthy environment.

6. INTIMIDATION

People follow because…
- ◊ they are afraid not to.
- ◊ they may not be physically pushed but are emotionally pushed.
- ◊ they want to avoid being fired, attacked, hurt, embarrassed, confronted, punished.

This is the second lowest form of power. It's used when ideas run out and quick action is needed.

7. FORCE

People follow because…
- ◊ they are threatened.
- ◊ they are overpowered by someone else.
- ◊ they move unwillingly.

Both people and countries exercise this kind of power. It is the lowest form of power.

Group Up

Can your group come up with one person in history for each path given who used this path as their means to power?

What was the result?

The Honor of Shining Boots

It was a hard blow for Samuel Brengle when he found himself in a cellar shining the boots of other cadets. He had not expected this. When signing up for the Salvation Army, Brengle had expected to be thrown immediately into evangelistic ministry. Instead, he found himself surrounded by a pile of black, muddy shoes. It was a sharp temptation for Brengle to see this as a blatant waste of his time and talent. He asked Jesus if he was burying his talents. He wondered if he was wasting his time in the Salvation Army.

It was down in that cellar that he saw a vision. In it, Jesus, the central figure, was washing the disciples' feet! Jesus, the One who had existed in the glories of the Everlasting Father, was now kneeling at the feet of grimy, uneducated fishermen . . . all to wash their feet!

With this change of mind, Brengle's heart bowed low. He pledged to the Savior: "Lord, you washed their feet, so I will shine their boots. And with that, he went forth, polishing boots with an enthusiasm in his arms, a song on his lips, and a peace in his heart.

Years later he recorded: "I had fellowship with Jesus every morning that week while down in the cellar . . . My prayer was, 'Dear Lord, let me serve the servants of Jesus. That is sufficient for me!'"[4]

Assess Yourself...

Let's review....Fill in the key words that describe what a servant leader is.

Christ-like servants...

1. Are motivated by _____ to serve others.

2. Possess a _____ that frees them to minister effectively.

3. _____ servant ministry to others.

4. _____ servant ministry from others.

5. Want nothing to interfere with their _____ with Jesus.

6. Teach servanthood by their _____.

7. Live a _____ life.

8. Live their lives _____ the philosophy of the world.

In which of the eight areas do you need to do some refining to truly be practicing the art of the basin and towel?

Are you a leader that thinks horizontally or vertically? How can you think more like Jesus in regard to leadership?

How can you become a better servant leader? Is there anything in yourself or habits you have that you need to die to in order to fully serve others in your leadership?

Application

Who is one person you find difficult to serve? Write their name down. Then, list three ways you could serve them this week.

What will you do? When will you do it? Who will hold you accountable?

You Can Be A People Person

CULTIVATING YOUR RELATIONAL SKILLS

The entire law is summed up in a single command: "Love your neighbor as yourself."
Gal. 5:14

Quick Thinking

I heard a funny story about a student who had the ability to sweet talk his way out of any difficult situation. Regardless of how sticky the conflict, his silver tongue was able to negotiate the way through the maze and come out unscathed.

As a freshman in college, he was working at a grocery store. A woman approached him wanting to buy half a head of lettuce. He looked at her funny and said: "You can't buy half a head of lettuce, you gotta buy the whole head. That's just plain stupid!" The woman got offended and demanded she talk to his manager. When he got to the back room to ask the manager to come out, the woman was right behind him. The young student had no idea. He belted out: "Sir, some old bat on aisle seven wants to buy a half of a head of lettuce! Isn't that the dumbest thing you ever heard?" The manager's eyes grew large because he could see the lady standing right behind his young employee. However, seeing his manager's eyes get big, he quickly recognized what was happening. He turned to the lady, and said, "And this beautiful lady would like to buy the other half of the lettuce."

She walked away happy. The manager was impressed. "I am amazed. I have never seen anyone talk their way out of a sticky situation so quickly! Where are you from anyway?" Without thinking, the student replied, "I'm from Toronto. The land of beautiful hockey players and ugly women!" Suddenly, the manager stepped back and retorted: "I beg your pardon! My wife is from Toronto!" But without a moment's hesitation, the employee smiled and asked, "Oh really? Which team did she play for?"

Don't you wish handling people were that easy? Unfortunately, it isn't. Because people are fragile and volatile, building people skills into your leadership needs to be a priority.

Leadership is Relationships

Years ago, Christian scholars met together at a summit in an attempt to distill the Christian faith into a single, defining phrase. They took it one more step. They summarized our faith into a single word. The one word definition they agreed upon was this:

Christianity = Relationships

Remember the two greatest commands? Jesus said life is all about loving God with all of our heart and loving our neighbor as we love ourselves. It's all about relationships. A vertical relationship and a horizontal relationship. Jesus did not say, "Do this in remembrance of my doctrine." He said, "Do this in remembrance of me." He did not say, "What do they say about my teachings?" but rather, "Who do they say that I am?" And, He did not say, "By this all men will know you are my disciples – that you memorize 50 verses of Scripture." Instead, He said they would know we are His disciples by the loving relationships we build!

Relationships will make or break a leader over time. If the leader fails to recognize their importance, he or she will eventually learn this lesson in a painful fashion.

The Advantage of a Frog

Someone once said, "The frog has a wonderful advantage in life. He can eat whatever bugs him!" Wouldn't it be nice if we could rid ourselves of the things that bug us as we lead others. You will find that people can be your greatest ally and your deepest curse. Stop and think about your situation. What really bugs you about people?

FOUR FOUNDATIONS

There are four foundations that you must understand as a leader if you desire to develop good people skills. These foundations give the perspective a leader should carry into his or her leadership when dealing with people.

- ⋄ People are an organization's most appreciable asset.

- ⋄ A leader's most important asset is people skills.

- ⋄ A good leader can lead various groups because leadership is about people.

- ⋄ You can have people skills and not be a good leader, but you cannot be a good leader without people skills.

The Best Medicine

William Osler was a physician until his death, at age 70, in 1919. Some called him the greatest physician that ever lived. He was a leader from the days he was a student. He was a natural ringleader and was the most influential student in his school. He always showed an uncanny ability with people. Everything Osler did spoke of the importance of building relationships. As a professional, he founded the Association of American Physicians. As a teacher, he changed the way medical schools functioned. His passion was to teach doctors compassion. He modeled this as he called upon patients in their homes during the 1918 epidemic of influenza pneumonia.

When he died, a colleague said of him: "So passed into history, untimely, even though he had attained the allotted span, the greatest physician in history… And above all, it is as a friend that during his lifetime we regarded Osler as one who possessed the genius of friendship to a greater degree than anyone of our generation. It was his wonderful interest in all of us that was the outstanding feature… It was from his humanity, his extraordinary interest in his fellows, that all his other powers seemed to flow."[1]

Group Up

Here's a question for discussion. What really bugs you about people?

Think about your top responses, then talk it over.

"The most important single ingredient to the formula for success is knowing how to get along with people."
Teddy Roosevelt

Reflect and Respond...

Henry Ford once said, "You can take my factories and burn up my buildings, but give me my people and I'll build the business right back again." Do you agree with his assessment that people are the essential component to any organization? ❑ yes ❑ no ❑ maybe Why or why not?

Reflect

and

Respond

"You can take my factories and burn up my buildings, but give me my people and I'll build the business right back again."
Henry Ford

Luke 10:30-37

"'There was once a man traveling from Jerusalem to Jericho. On the way he was attacked by robbers. They took his clothes, beat him up, and went off leaving him half-dead. Luckily, a priest was on his way down the same road, but when he saw him he angled across to the other side. Then a Levite religious man showed up; he also avoided the injured man.

A Samaritan traveling the road came on him. When he saw the man's condition, his heart went out to him. He gave him first aid, disinfecting and bandaging his wounds. Then he lifted him on to his donkey, led him to an inn, and made him comfortable. In the morning he took out two silver coins and gave them to the innkeeper, saying, 'Take good care of him. If it costs any more, put it on my bill - I'll pay you on my way back.'

What do you think? Which of the three became a neighbor to the man attacked by robbers?'

'The one who treated him kindly,' the religion scholar responded.

Jesus said, 'Go and do the same'" (The Message).

The story of the "Good Samaritan" illustrates how different people view a person by the way they see themselves:

The Robbers	The Priests	The Samaritan
Used People	Law Keepers	Despised
Manipulative	Pure	Ignored
They saw the man as a victim to exploit.	They saw the man as a problem to avoid.	He saw the man as a person to be loved.

Group Up

Discuss Henry Ford's statement.

Why are people so crucial to a leader?

Reflect and Respond...

As a leader, you will be tempted to see people with all three of these perspectives! As you read through this passage, with whom do you identify? Why?

❑ The Robbers _____

_____

❑ The Priests _____

_____

❑ The Samaritan _____

_____

How can you avoid following in the footsteps of the first two groups of people?

As a leader, you will have the opportunity to do all three of these: exploit, avoid, and love people. The goal is to attempt to identify with a person's needs and allow "your heart to go out to them." Oftentimes the people who are the most difficult to love simply have deep wounds that need healing and care.

Define It

If you think about what it means to be a spiritual leader, it is all about relationships.

I define spiritual leadership as:

One who assumes responsibility for the health and development of their relationships.

Reflect and Respond...

Would you agree with this definition? ❑ yes ❑ no ❑ in part
What do you understand spiritual leadership to be?

Do you assume responsibility for the health and development of any of your relationships? Are you functioning as a spiritual leader right now? List ways others would see you as a leader on your campus.

> "'What do you think? Which of the three became a neighbor to the man attacked by robbers?' 'The one who treated him kindly,' the religion scholar responded. Jesus said, 'Go and do the same.'"
> Luke 10:36-37
> (The Message)

What's Your Struggle?

In assuming responsibility for a relationship, it is helpful to understand why people struggle with relationships. It won't come as a surprise that these struggles differ for men and women.

Why Men Struggle with Relationships

1. Men have been trained for their WORKPLACE, not for their relationships.

2. Men draw their IDENTITY from "achievement" more than relationships.

3. Our culture has given us a faulty VIEW of masculinity and relationships.

4. Men are often driven to push for quick RESULTS and fail to enjoy the process.

5. Men often don't feel safe being VULNERABLE and revealing feelings.

6. Men are INDEPENDENT and sometimes feel they really don't need others.

Why Women Struggle with Relationships

1. Because women bond so quickly, they often take on TOO MANY relationships at too deep of a level.

2. Relationships can be a source of COMPETITION and comparison.

3. Since relationships are so important, women can be tempted to CONTROL them.

4. Women have seen poor MODELS of healthy spiritual leadership and relationships.

5. Women may depend on human relationships to do what only GOD can do.

Reflect and Respond...

As a man or woman, can you identify with these struggles? Which ones do you find you wrestle with the most in relationships?

What can you do to help minimize these?

Reflect
and
Respond

Group Up

Talk about the different struggles men and women have with relationships.

Share ways to help overcome these struggles.

WHAT EVERY LEADER SHOULD KNOW ABOUT PEOPLE

Hopefully by this point, you agree with me that your ability to care for your relationships will make or break you as a leader on the campus and elsewhere. Since relationships are so vital to being an effective leader, here are ten important things that you as a leader will need to know about the people you are leading.

1. People are Insecure. Give them Confidence.

We all know what it is like to be insecure. Whether over our looks, our intelligence, or our skills and talents, each one of us has struggled with feeling insecure about something. Most people are insecure. And most insecure people are looking for security. Here is the important point for you to realize as a leader: a secure atmosphere is provided by secure and confident people. If you want to build security in others, you will need to be secure and confident yourself. Now I am not talking about a false confidence, where you fake it just enough to hide your insecurity, or an arrogant, prideful feeling of superiority. I am talking about a genuine confidence where you know your worth lies in your identity in Christ, not in other people or in what you do. You know what God has called you to do and are confident in His ability to equip you to carry out that calling. You are able to lift others up with encouragement and praise, rather than feeling the need to raise yourself above them. You must CARE for each person:

> A secure atmosphere is provided by secure and confident people. If you want to build security in others, you will need to be secure and confident yourself.

Give Them Confidence

Communicate
Appreciate
Recognize
Empower

KEY PRINCIPLE

Hurting people hurt people.
Secure people offer security to people.

A Secure Command

During 1989 and 1990, the Soviet Union was dismantled. Soviet leader Michel Gorbechav was out and Boris Yeltsin was in as president of Russia. However, there were days in Moscow when a peaceful transition looked very unlikely. Yeltsin demonstrated what it took to win the people of Moscow - and beyond.

One day, a tank rolled into Moscow, armed and ready to fire. When Yeltsin saw it, he ran out to it, signaled for it to halt, then climbed up and opened the hatch. When he saw two soldiers inside, he exclaimed, "I am so glad you are here! I have been looking for you for some time. Thank you for coming. Here is how you can help me." He then laid out the best ways they could help the cause of his presidency.

Later, those two men stated, "We were amazed at his confidence. When we entered the city, the military was in disarray. We had not yet made up our mind who's side we were on. But when Yeltsin demonstrated his confidence and a definite need, we determined to help him." Wow! Most people are looking for a secure leader to follow.

Reflect and Respond...

How secure are you?

How can you give other people confidence?

Reflect

and

Respond

2. People Like to Feel Special. Honor Them.

Mark Twain once said, "One compliment can keep me going for a whole month." We all like to be praised and complimented. Everyone likes to feel special. As a leader, you will need to do this for your people.

To help you in doing this, here are some pointers on giving compliments:
- ◇ Make them Sincere – Be genuine and authentic about what you say.
- ◇ Make them Specific – Be very pointed and specific about what you say.
- ◇ Make them Public – Share this honoring word in front of others.
- ◇ Make them Personal – Get beyond general gratitude; speak personally to them.

KEY PRINCIPLE

To deal with yourself, use your head.
To deal with others, use your heart.

The Blue Ribbon Experiment

A professor in New York decided to spend a day, expressing how much her students meant to her and how they made a difference to the class. She had each of them walk to the front of the class for a blue ribbon and a word of encouragement. Although the exercise was foreign to some of the students, every one of them enjoyed a moment of praise and recognition.

Next, the teacher told her students she wanted to continue this experiment. She gave all of her students extra blue ribbons and told them to honor someone in their life, whom they appreciated. Afterward, they were to give an extra blue ribbon to that person, and encourage them to do the same. Then her students were to report the results to the class.

One student had an unbelievable experience. He went to honor a businessman, who had mentored him and helped him prepare for his career. He gave the man a ribbon, and asked if he would pass it on to someone he appreciated. Later, the man walked in to his supervisor's office and gave him the ribbon and expressed his gratitude for how he had impacted his life. This shocked the supervisor, as everyone knew him to be an angry tyrant as a boss. He thanked his colleague and accepted his extra ribbon to pass on to a person he appreciated and wanted to honor.

On his way home, the supervisor considered to whom he would give his blue ribbon. When he arrived home, he entered his son's room and spoke to him. "Son, I know I get mad at you often for not cleaning your room, or not doing the chores around the house. I also know I get so busy, I fail to interact with you and tell you how much I care about you. So tonight, I just wanted to tell you how much you mean to me. Outside of your mother, you are the most important person in the world to me. I love you."

The boy couldn't even look at his father. He buried his head in his pillow and began to sob. He cried for several minutes before he could regain his composure. Then, he attempted to speak. "Dad, I have never heard you say those things to me before. I never knew how you felt about me. When you walked in tonight, I was feeling totally alone and I was planning to commit suicide tomorrow because I felt no one really cared. Now I guess I don't have to."[2]

We never know how much a word of affirmation and honor will do for someone else.

Reflect and Respond...

Think of specific ways you make someone feel special.

Who is one person in your life who needs to be honored by you? Make a list of what you can do with your "blue ribbons."

1.
2.
3.
4.
5.

3. People Look for a Better Tomorrow. Show Them Hope.

Everyone lives for something better to come. Where there is no hope in the future, there is no power in the present. The pastors of the largest churches in the U.S. were asked years ago what their main goal was on Sunday morning. One common thread emerged. Each of them said that their chief goal every Sunday was to offer hope to their people. As a leader, this should be one of your chief goals.

Helpless...Hopeless...

There is an alarming percentage of students, between the ages of 16 and 24, that commit suicide each year in the U.S. On the occasions when a suicide note is found, it almost always expresses helplessness and hopelessness: life wasn't worth living without meaning and purpose. Where there is no hope in the future, there is no power in the present. People can live a few minutes without air. They can live a few days without water. They can live several weeks without food. But take away their hope, and the dying process begins almost immediately.

KEY PRINCIPLE

The key to today is the belief in tomorrow.

Reflect and Respond...

Why do you think it is important to show hope to the people you lead? How can you do this? Make your list. Now, share it with someone who also made a list.

Reflect

and

Respond

4. People Need to be Understood. Listen to Them.

When a person comes to talk to you about a problem, usually they are looking for someone to listen to them and show understanding; they are not necessarily looking for advice. This simple act of listening could prevent problems in the future. As an old Cherokee saying goes, "Listen to the whispers and you won't have to hear the screams."

Listen

to

Them

KEY PRINCIPLE

If a leader is to connect with others, he or she must understand the "key" to their heart.

The Doll Broke...

One afternoon Katie asked her dad if she could play with her friend next door. Her dad replied it would be fine as long as she was home by 6:00 pm. Well, 6:00 pm came and left and Katie was nowhere to be found. Dad grew a little upset when he had to call and ask that Katie be sent home.

When she got home a half hour later, her dad said, "Didn't you hear me tell you to come home by 6:00?"

"Yes," Katie replied, "But my friend's doll broke."

Her dad mellowed a bit. "Oh, I see. And, you stayed to help her fix it?"

"No," Katie whispered. "I stayed to help her cry."

Sometimes, as we lead people, we discover that people don't need us to fix anything. They need us to help them cry. They need someone to understand them and identify with where they are.

Reflect and Respond...

As a college student, are you a good listener? How can you improve your listening skills?

Reflect

To know the key to someone's heart, you need to know what they talk about and cry about, what they laugh about and dream about, what they plan about and sing about. How can you get to know the people you lead so you know these things about them?

Respond

Group Up

Share with the group your thoughts on how to be a good listener.

What listening skills have you developed that have made you a better listener?

5. People Lack Direction. Navigate for Them.

Harold Kushner writes: "Our souls are not hungry for fame, comfort, wealth or power. Those rewards create almost as many problems as they solve. Our souls are hungry for meaning, for the sense that we have figured out how to live so that our lives matter, so that the world will at least be a little bit different for our having passed through it." All people want to live a life of meaning and purpose. As a leader, you will need to help provide the direction and guidance for people to accomplish this.

Navigate for Them

KEY PRINCIPLE

Most people can steer their ship as long as someone helps to chart the course.

Reflect and Respond...

What will be the challenges for you in providing direction and charting the course for people?

Reflect

and

Respond

"Our souls are hungry for meaning, for the sense that we have figured out how to live so that our lives matter, so that the world will at least be a little bit different for our having passed through it."

Harold Kushner

6. People are Selfish. Speak to Their Needs First.

Whether you like it or not, most people are selfish. Their world revolves around their own needs and wants. They are typically asking, "What's in it for me?" We must connect with them by starting where they are. Then, we can help them grow into the people they should be.

This is the common mindset:
Most people think...
Their situation is unique.
Their problems are the biggest.
Their faults ought to be overlooked.
Their time is most precious.

This needs to be a leader's response:
Leaders must...
Put their people first.
Know their people's needs.
See the total picture.
Love people enough to help them grow.

Speak to Their Needs First

KEY PRINCIPLE

People will meet the needs of others when they feel their own needs will be cared for.

Reflect and Respond...

What are ways you can...
Put your people first?

Reflect

and

Respond

Know your people's needs?

What does it mean to...
See the total picture?

Love people enough to help them grow?

7. People get Emotionally Low. Encourage Them.

Years ago an experiment was conducted to measure people's capacity to endure pain. How long could a bare-footed person stand in a bucket of ice water? It was discovered that when there was someone else present offering encouragement and support, the person standing in the ice water could tolerate the pain twice as long as when there was no one present. Encouragement can make a person go twice as far as they could go alone.

KEY PRINCIPLE

What gets rewarded gets done.

Students Who Were on Empty

Group Up

Talk about what might have prevented the students in the story to the right from committing the acts they did.

How can you help identify and encourage people around you who are emotionally low?

Many high school students have endured a "grim rite of passage" into adulthood, during their teen years. Over the last seven years, a series of shootings took place on campuses in Oregon, Arkansas, Kentucky, Georgia, and Mississippi. In 1999, the worst of this series of massacres occurred at Columbine High School, where two outcasts murdered fourteen students and one teacher. In 2001, a fifteen-year old freshman, Charles Andrew Williams, who was often teased by his classmates, took a pistol and began shooting people at Santana High School in Santee, CA. Before he finished, two people were killed and fourteen were injured. He smiled as he fired the gun.

While I believe these shootings have galvanized the Millennial Generations as a whole, they illustrate the fact that some students still feel like outsiders, even in the pluralistic world we live in today. The only way these students felt they could deal with it was to destroy their lives and the lives of others. They gained a sadistic satisfaction in taking out their unhappiness by firing a gun.

I believe they needed a leader to enter their life prior to the tragedies. They needed someone to look past their faults and see their needs. They needed a person to recognize their emotional "tank" was low, speak into their life and recognize the contribution they could make to their world. Could you be this person even as a college student giving time to work with youth in a church or some other type youth organization. I think you can.

Reflect and Respond...

How can you provide emotional support and encouragement to your followers and others in need? Make a list and come back to it from time to time to make sure you are doing these things.

8. People Want to Associate with Success. Help Them Win.

Question: What do these things have in common?

| High morale | Enthusiasm | Fun |
| Optimism | Energy | Momentum |

Answer: Winning

Help
Them
Win

Everyone likes to win...to be a part of the winning team. Help your people feel successful. That will take them and you far.

When Kevin Won...

If you had to choose one word to describe Kevin, it might have been the word "slow." He was in all the remedial groups at school. He never finished first in a school race. He didn't learn his ABCs as fast as the other kids. However, Kevin loved life and people, so when his pastor, Randy, decided to start a church basketball team, Kevin begged to join.

Both Kevin and his team loved basketball, but just loving the game doesn't help you win. Although Kevin watched most of the games from the bench, shouting encouragement to his teammates, they lost every game that year, except for one - the night it snowed and the other team never showed up for the game. When the season ended, Kevin's team drew the unfortunate spot of playing against the first place team in the tournament - the tall, undefeated first place team. The game went as everyone expected. By the fourth quarter, the other team was whipping Kevin's team by almost forty points.

It was then, that one of Kevin's teammates called timeout. When the team got to the bench, this player softly said: "Coach, I realize this is probably our last game this season. And I was thinking...um...Kevin has been on the bench most of the time and he never got to make a basket all season. Coach, I think we should let Kevin make a basket." With the game out of reach, the coach decided it would be okay. Kevin was told to stand at the free throw line and wait for a pass. Then, he was to shoot.

When his team got the ball, Kevin launched a shot. It bounced and missed. Number 17 from the other team rebounded the ball, and took it down for another two points. When Kevin's team got the ball, they passed it to him and he shot again. Another miss. Again, number 17 grabbed the rebound, and scored. This pattern continued a few more times until number 17 grew wise. After rebounding the ball, instead of leading a fast break to his own basket, he passed the ball back to Kevin, who shot and missed again. However, at this point, everyone on the court began to join in, passing the ball back to Kevin. And Kevin just kept shooting. It took the fans just a bit longer to figure out what was happening, but eventually everyone was standing, clapping and cheering for Kevin to make a basket. Soon, the whole gym broke out into a chant: Ke-vin! Ke-vin! Ke-vin! Coach Randy noticed the referees had even stopped the clock and were leaning against the scoring table clapping for Kevin. The whole world, it seemed, was stopped, waiting and wanting for Kevin. Finally, after an infinite amount of tries, the ball took a miraculous bounce and went in. At that second, Kevin's arms shot into the air as he shouted, "I won!"

Soon, the remaining seconds ticked off the clock and the first place team remained undefeated. But on that night, everyone left the game feeling like they had won. I believe everyone under your leadership needs a moment where they are honored and feel as though the whole team is behind them.

KEY PRINCIPLE

People may root for the underdog –
but it's because they want him to win!

Reflect and Respond...

What would count as "wins" among other students on your campus? How can you help other students feel successful?

9. People Want Meaningful Relationships. Provide Community.

God's word is all about community - from the garden of Eden in the beginning, to the city of God in the end. Help connect people to one another.

Real Life

CHURCH SURVEY:

Q: Why did you join the church?
A: The pastor

Q: If the pastor left, would you leave too?
A: No, because I've found friends at the church.

Lyle Schaller has done extensive research that shows the more friendships a person has in a congregation, the less likely he or she is to become inactive or leave. In contrast, I once read about a survey where they asked 400 church dropouts why they left their churches. Over 75% of the respondents said: I didn't feel anyone cared whether I was there or not.

KEY PRINCIPLE

Apply the 101% Principle:
Find the 1% you have in common with someone,
and give it 100% of your attention.

Can you think of a situation where you became involved in something for one reason but stayed with it because of the relationships you formed? Write about it.

Reflect

What are ways you can provide community for other students?

and

Respond

> "Preach the Gospel at all times. If necessary, use words."
> St. Francis of Assisi

10. People Seek Models. Be an Example.

The early followers of St. Francis of Assisi wanted to know what to do when they went out into the streets to minister. "Preach the Gospel at all times," St. Francis advised. "If necessary, use words."

Be an Example

Nothing can take the place of a leader setting the example for others. People don't necessarily do what they hear, they do what they see. People emulate models. They would rather see a sermon than hear one any day.

Who's Your Hero?

Andrew Leary did some research as a college student on the problem of hunger in the U.S. He discovered that hunger was not only a problem in America, but in his own hometown. When he began to talk about it, everyone agreed, but no one acted. That's when Andrew decided to set an example. He assessed the scope of the problem by organizing a one-day "Harvest Festival" where students handed out 1,000 pounds of food along with a survey. The results proved that he was right. There was a real problem with hunger right under their noses.

Andrew put a team together to come up with a plan and to raise money. He became a spokesman for a task force in the community. He shared his vision with civic groups, churches, community groups, the media and the county planning board. Finally he had the support needed to begin a ministry to the hungry. He led the way to raise $35,000 to operate a facility, Harvest House. He said later, "I realized that although I'm just a student, I have the vision and the ability to change lives. I learned that standing up for what you believe in is not always easy, but through perseverance you can reach your goal." All his community needed was someone to set an example.

KEY PRINCIPLE

People do what people see.

Group Up

Discuss the ways to do as St. Francis of Assisi instructed his followers: "Preach the Gospel at all times. If necessary use words."

How do you share your faith without words?

Is your life something that others could and should model? Why or why not?

Reflect

What do you need to do to become a better example to others?

and

Respond

Let's Review...

Before we move on, let's review the ten things every leader should know about people. Fill in the key words that illustrate good people skills.

1. People are insecure. Give them _____.

2. People like to feel special. _____ them.

3. People look for a better tomorrow. Show them _____.

4. People need to be understood. _____ to them.

5. People lack direction. _____ for them.

6. People are selfish. Speak to their _____ _____.

7. People get emotionally low. _____ them.

8. People want to associate with success. Help them _____.

9. People want meaningful relationships. Provide _____.

10. People Seek Models. Be an _____.

In which areas are you weak? What steps might you take to improve your people skills in this area?

Spiritual Leadership Checklist

The following qualities mark a true spiritual leader. They are inward qualities that you can evaluate your life against. Rank yourself on a scale of 1-10 on these traits:

SCORE

1. INITIATIVE ( )
- ◇ I give direction to the primary relationships of my life.
- ◇ I take responsibility for the health of my relationships.
- ◇ I initiate spiritual dialogue with vulnerability and humility.

2. INTIMACY ( )
- ◇ I experience intimacy with God through personal worship and study time.
- ◇ I experience intimacy with my primary relationships in open conversation.
- ◇ I experience relationships where I am fully known without fear of rejection.

3. INFLUENCE ( )
- ◇ I exercise Biblical influence within my relationships.
- ◇ I develop, encourage, and facilitate growth in my primary relationships.
- ◇ I am a "giver", a generous contributor in relationships.

4. INTEGRITY ( )
- ◇ I lead a life of integrity and honesty that is above reproach.
- ◇ I'm not ashamed of my "private world," who I am when no one is looking.
- ◇ I avoid hypocrisy because I live by what I believe wherever I go.

5. IDENTITY ( )
- ◇ I am secure in who I am in Christ.
- ◇ I have a healthy, biblical self-image that prevents a defensive attitude.
- ◇ I have developed a mature statement of purpose for my life.

6. INNER-CHARACTER ( )
- ◇ I exhibit the fruit of the Spirit in my life, which includes self-discipline.
- ◇ I am a Spirit-filled, Spirit-led believer.
- ◇ I maintain control by submission to God's authority first, then human authority.

How do You Rank?

Add up your scores from each quality. How did you do?

45-60: You are functioning as a strong and healthy spiritual leader. Continue to cultivate these qualities in your life.

25-44: You are on your way to becoming an effective spiritual leader. Assess which qualities you are lacking and what you can do to strengthen these in your life.

6-24: You have some areas of growth to address before you are ready to take on the role of a spiritual leader. Look over the six qualities listed above and the aspects given in each. Determine what needs to be done to grow in these areas.

Assess Yourself

Relationships are crucial to leadership. Without cultivating strong relationships with people you will not survive as a leader. With that in mind, how are you at this point in your life with cultivating relationships?

Do you have strong people skills? Check one: ❑ yes ❑ no ❑ still growing

Examine the "Spiritual Leadership Checklist" one more time. List the areas you are weak.

What do you struggle with most in relationships?

How can you begin to overcome these struggles?

Remember, Christianity is all about relationships: our relationship with God and others. Nothing is greater than these two things. Commit now to strengthening all your relationships, first your relationship with God, and second to those around you. In doing these two things, it will be the best way to ensure your success as a leader.

Guided Prayer

Dear God, it is easy to love people who are loveable.

Help me reach out to the unloveable - to those who are hurting, wounded and have put up walls to protect themselves.

Help me break down the barriers with each person I encounter so that I might be Your instrument of grace, mercy and love in their life.

Shape my heart after Your own - a heart that loves and cares for people.

Amen.

Application

What is one step you will take as a result of this chapter? When will you take it? Who will hold you accountable? Review this chapter and think about what specifically you can do to take a step toward implementing the lessons in this session. Write out what you will do and when you will do it. Ask one person in the group to hold you accountable during the week. Be ready to share with the group next time you meet what step you took and anything you learned or gained from it.

CONGRATULATIONS!

You have diligently worked through this book

and are on the path to becoming a person

of influence for the Kingdom of God.

We hope that you have gained new insights into yourself

and a better understanding of leadership.

But this is only the beginning. Please read on to discover

other ways that you can grow as a leader.

A Word About
EQUIP

EQUIP is a non-profit Christian organization devoted to the development of Christ-like leaders in the most influential and neglected places of our world. We believe that everything rises and falls on leadership. We partner with ministries, churches, and schools in three key areas: the international community, the urban community, and among students in the academic community. This collegiate workbook is part of our partnership in the academic arena.

Developing leaders among college students allows us to invest in tomorrow's leaders today. Here are a few of the resources that we currently offer:

• Leadership Conferences

The Leadership Forums are 1-2 day training events tailor-made to the needs of your campus ministry. They can be profiled as outreach events on your campus for fraternities, sororities, RA's, student government, and more. The conferences serve as a catalyst to build hunger for further personal leadership development.

• Mentoring Groups

The Leadership Exchange contains a year's worth of leadership cassette tapes, taught by Dr. John C. Maxwell, to spark discussion and application in monthly mentoring groups. In addition to the tapes, student handbooks and facilitator's guides are provided. Along with this tool, we offer "Portrait of a leader," a series of discussion guides on leadership. Our hope is to provide support, interaction, accountability, and to foster a leadership culture within your ministry through these tools.

• Video Curriculum

The Leadership Journey is designed to furnish ongoing, systematic leadership training for students. The video curriculum is divided into 72 12-minute segments to be viewed in class and then discussed. The lectures cover the "21 Irrefutable Laws of Leadership" and are taught by Dr. John C. Maxwell and Dr. Tim Elmore. It is crafted to be used in a classroom setting along with assignments and reading.

• Resources

The Leadership Library represents a fourth component in our partnership. EQUIP offers a battery of books, tapes, videos, and training manuals for leaders and potential leaders to enhance your leadership growth. The resources cover subjects including leadership, mentoring, spiritual growth, people skills, priorities, vision, staff development, and more. These have been discounted for campus workers and college students.

• Leadership Academy

The Leadership Academy is a two-week institute for student interns. It is designed to develop leadership qualities and skills through adventure learning, reading, interviews, field trips, mentors, small groups, and equipping seminars. For information, check out our Web site at www.leadership-academy.org.

Visit EQUIP at www.equiporg.org

A Word About
National Collegiate Ministry (NCM)

National Collegiate Ministry is an arm of LifeWay Christian Resources of the Southern Baptist Convention. With over 80 years of ministry on the college campus, our ministry speaks to and for hundreds of thousands college students each year. We have five main objectives in ministering to collegians. They are: Bible study; Evangelism; Leadership Development; Transformational Discipleship, and Christian service.

A spiritual strategy we use to develop collegiate leaders in churches and campus programs is called CrossSeekers.

CrossSeekers Covenant Living

Collegians across the country are taking the pledge to covenant living. Students are seeking to develop spiritual lives which exhibit the six CrossSeeker Covenant points. These are:

Integrity: I will seek to be a person of integrity (2 Timothy 2:15).
My attitudes and actions reveal my commitment to live the kind of life Christ modeled for me—to speak the truth in love, to stand firm in my convictions, and to be honest and trustworthy.

Witness: I will seek to speak and live a relevant, authentic, and consistent witness (1 Peter 3:15).
I will tell others the story of how Jesus changed my life, and I will seek to live a radically changed life each day. I will share the good news of Jesus Christ with courage and boldness.

Spiritual Growth: I will seek to pursue consistent spiritual growth (Colossians 2:6-7).
The Christian life is a continuing journey, and I am committed to a consistent, personal relationship with Jesus Christ, to faithful study of His Word, and to regular corporate spiritual growth through the ministry of the New Testament church.

I will seek opportunities to serve in Christ's name (Luke 4:18-19).
I believe that God desires to draw all people into a loving, redeeming relationship with Him. As His disciple, I will give myself to be His hands to reach others in ministry and missions.

I will seek to honor my body as the temple of God, dedicated to a lifestyle of purity (I Corinthians 6:19-20).
Following the example of Christ, I will keep my body healthy and strong, avoiding temptations and destructive personal vices. I will honor the gift of life by keeping myself sexually pure and free from addictive drugs.

I will seek to be godly in all things, Christlike in all relationships (Colossians 3:12-14).
In every relationship and in every situation, I will seek to live as Christ would. I will work to heal brokenness, to value each person as a child of God, to avoid petty quarrels and harsh word, to let go of bitterness and resentment that hinder genuine Christian love.

CrossSeeker Resources

For each point of the covenant, we have Christian resources written for the covenant for college students. To obtain a catalog of these resources, call 1-615-251-2777. To order a CrossSeeker resource, call 1-800-458-2772; fax 615-251-5933; email: customerservice@lifeway.com or visit the LifeWay Christian Store serving you.

CrossSeekers Covenant Conferences

These conferences are held throughout the year and throughout the country. For the one closest to you, call 1-615-251-2777. This conference time is designed to assist you in becoming the Christian leader on campus God wants you to be.

CrossSeekers information

For more information on CrossSeekers Covenant Living, contact us at 615-251-2777 or on the web at www.crossseekers.org.

Authentic Influence Footnotes

Session 1
1. Barna, George, *The Power of Vision* (Ventura: Regal Books, 1992).

Session 4
1. *Mr. Holland's Opus* (Hollywood Pictures, written by Patrick Sheane Duncan, directed by Stephen Herek, 1996).
2. Maxwell, John, *The 21 Irrefutable Laws of leadership*, Nashville, Thomas Nelson, Inc., 1998
3. Ibid.
4. Skinner, Betty, *DAWS*, Wheaton, NavPress, 1995.

Session 5
1. Covey, Stephen, *Principle Centered Leadership*, New York, Simon and Shuster, 1990, p. 58.
2. Blair, Charles, *The Man Who Could Do No Wrong* (Wheaton, Tyndale House Publishers, 1989).

Session 6
1. Barna, George, *The Power of Vision*.
2. Dawson, John, Taking Our Cities for God (Creation House, Strang Communications Co., 1989).

Session 7
1. Nouwen, Henri, J.M., *In The Name of Jesus* (New York, CrossRoad Publishing, 1989).
2. Ibid.
3. Greissman, Gene, *The Words Lincoln Lived By* (New York, Simon and Schuster, 1997).
4. Hall, Clarence Wl, *Portrait of A Prophet* (The Salvation Army, Inc., 1993).

Session 8
1. Maxwell, John C, the 21 Indespensable Qualities of A Leader (Nashville, Thoman Nelson, 1999).
2. Canfied, Jack and Mark Victor Hansen, *Chicken Soup For The Soul* (Deerfield Beach, FL, Health Communications, 1996).